ON THE PRINCIPLE

PRINCIPLE

OF

SUFFICIENT

REASON

Titles on Metaphysics and Epistemology in Prometheus's Great Books in Philosophy Series

Aristotle, *De Anima*

Aristotle, *The Metaphysics*

Francis Bacon, *Essays*

George Berkeley, *Three Dialogues Between Hylas and Philonous*

W. K. Clifford, *The Ethics of Belief and Other Essays*

René Descartes, *Discourse on Method* and *The Meditations*

John Dewey, *How We Think*

John Dewey, *The Influence of Darwin on Philosophy and Other Essays*

Epicurus, *The Essential Epicurus: Letters, Principal Doctrines, Vatican Sayings, and Fragments*

Sidney Hook, *The Quest for Being*

David Hume, *An Enquiry Concerning Human Understanding*

David Hume, *Treatise of Human Nature*

William James, *The Meaning of Truth*

William James, *Pragmatism*

Immanuel Kant, *Critique of Judgment*

Immanuel Kant, *Critique of Practical Reason*

Immanuel Kant, *Critique of Pure Reason*

Gottfried Wilhelm Leibniz, *Discourse on Metaphysics* and *The Monadology*

John Locke, *An Essay Concerning Human Understanding*

George Herbert Mead, *The Philosophy of the Present*

Michel de Montaigne, *Essays*

Charles S. Peirce, *The Essential Writings*

Plato, *The Euthyphro, Apology, Crito,* and *Phaedo*

Plato, *Lysis, Phaedrus, Crito,* and *Symposium*

Bertrand Russell, *The Problems of Philosophy*

George Santayana, *The Life of Reason*

Arthur Schopenhauer, *On the Principle of Sufficient Reason*

Sextus Empiricus, *Outlines of Pyrrhonism*

Ludwig Wittgenstein, *Wittgenstein's Lectures: Cambridge, 1932–1935*

Alfred North Whitehead, *The Concept of Nature*

See the back of this volume for a complete list of titles in Prometheus's Great Books in Philosophy and Great Minds series.

ON THE PRINCIPLE

OF

SUFFICIENT REASON

Translated by Karl Hillebrand

ARTHUR SCHOPENHAUER

GREAT BOOKS IN PHILOSOPHY

 Prometheus Books

59 John Glenn Drive
Amherst, New York 14228-2197

Published 2006 by Prometheus Books

Inquiries should be addressed to
Prometheus Books
59 John Glenn Drive
Amherst, New York 14228–2197

716–691–0133 (x207). FAX: 716–564–2711.
WWW.PROMETHEUSBOOKS.COM

10 09 08 07 06   5 4 3 2 1

This is the 1891 fourth edition with emendations by the author.

Library of Congress Cataloging-in-Publication Data

Schopenhauer, Arthur, 1788–1860.
    [Über die vierfache Wurzel des Satzes vom zureichenden
Grunde. English]
    On the principle of sufficient reason / by Arthur Schopenhauer.
        p. cm.
    Translated by Mme. Karl Hillebrand.
    Originally published: On the fourfold root of the principle of
sufficient reason. Rev. London : G. Bell, 1891.
    Includes bibliographical references.
    ISBN 1–59102–383–1 (alk. paper)
    1. Sufficient reason. 2. Will. I. Hillebrand, Karl, Mme.
II. Title.

B3123.E5H6 2006
193—dc22

                                                    2005054975

Printed in the United States of America on acid-free paper

ARTHUR SCHOPENHAUER, the famous nineteenth-century German pessimist who expanded on the ideas of Plato and Immanuel Kant, wrote accessibly, leading his ideas to resonate with both philosophers and artists alike.

The son of Heinrich Floris Schopenhauer and Johanna Henriette Troisiener, Arthur was born in Danzig on February 22, 1788, just one month after English Romantic poet George Gordon, Lord Byron. A middle-class Dutch family involved in international trade, the Schopenhauers chose "Arthur" as their son's name because the appellation is spelled the same in English, French, and German. Once Prussia annexed Danzig in 1793, the Schopenhauer family moved first to Hamburg, then Arthur spent much of his youth living throughout Europe, learning many languages. Although his father prepared him to inherit the family mercantile business, Arthur Schopenhauer found that the scholarly life suited him perfectly. After Heinrich's 1805 death, Johanna moved her family from Hamburg to Weimar, where Johanna, an author herself, befriended the writer Johann Wolfgang von Goethe.

Arthur Schopenhauer enrolled in the University of Göttingen and received his doctorate from the University of Jena in 1813. His dissertation, *The Fourfold Root of the Principle of Sufficient Reason*, explored the philosophical assumption that equates reality with rationality. According to Schopenhauer, in order for one to contemplate an explanation for a particular thing, one must assume that there is a subject (oneself) that thinks about the object (thing to be explained). Schopenhauer built his thesis on the work of Kant, who noted that humans cannot transcend themselves and therefore cannot satisfactorily answer metaphysical questions, and G. W. Leibniz, who first defined the principle of sufficient reason, which states that absolutely nothing exists that lacks an adequate reason for its existence.

Schopenhauer's most famous work, the two-volume *The*

World as Will and Representation, sprung from ideas put forth in *The Fourfold Root*. Schopenhauer's philosophical inquiries led him to embrace a pessimistic worldview—life is a meaningless struggle against the irrational impulses of the will. One could find some solace, however, through aesthetic perception, morality, and asceticism. With regard to the first, Schopenhauer considered artistic endeavors to be the communication of Platonic Ideas, with music as the highest of all art forms because of its instant objectification of the will. Schopenhauer's ideas influenced many literary figures—including Samuel Beckett, Joseph Conrad, Leo Tolstoy, W. B. Yeats, and Emile Zola—as well as musicians such as Johannes Brahms an Richard Wagner.

In the early 1920s, Schopenhauer began lecturing at the University of Berlin, purposely scheduling his classes concurrent with those of G. W. F. Hegel. Schopenhauer strongly disliked Hegel and his philosophy; the former felt that the latter tried to make up for a lack of content in his works by ensnaring the reader in meaningless jargon.

Schopenhauer left Berlin in 1831 to escape the threat of a cholera epidemic, eventually settling in Frankfurt, where he spent the rest of his life. By the mid-1850s, Schopenhauer gained the recognition that he had longed for when a review of his philosophical work appeared in the *Westminster Review*, which connected some of Schopenhauer's thought with that of Johann Gottlieb Fichte. Schopenhauer's health gradually deteriorated in 1860 until he died of natural causes on September 21 in Frankfurt. New editions of most of Schopenhauer's works began to appear in 1873.

Other works by Schopenhauer include *On Vision and Colors* (1816), *On the Will in Nature* (1836), *The Two Fundamental Problems of Ethics* (1839–40), *Parerga und Paralipomena* (1851), and *The Wisdom of Life and Counsels and Maxims* (1886).

CONTENTS

CHAP.   PAGE

Author's Preface ix

I.   Introduction 1

II.   General Survey of the Most Important Views
        Hitherto Held concerning the
        Principle of Sufficient Reason 6

III.   Insufficiency of the Old and Outlines
        of a New Demonstration 28

IV.   On the First Class of Objects for the
        Subject and That Form of the Principle of
        Sufficient Reason Which Predominates in It .. 31

V.   On the Second Class of Objects for the
Subject and That Form of the Principle
of Sufficient Reason Which
Predominates in It 114

VI.   On the Third Class of Objects for the
Subject and That Form of the Principle
of Sufficient Reason Which
Predominates in It 153

VII. On the Fourth Class of Objects for the
Subject and That Form of the Principle
of Sufficient Reason Which
Predominates in It 165

VIII. General Observations and Results 177

AUTHOR'S PREFACE
SECOND EDITION.

THIS treatise on Elementary Philosophy, which first appeared in the year 1813, when it procured for me the degree of doctor, afterwards became the substructure for the whole of my system. It cannot, therefore, be allowed to remain out of print, as has been the case, without my knowledge, for the last four years.

On the other hand, to send a juvenile work like this once more into the world with all its faults and blemishes, seemed to me unjustifiable. For I am aware that the time cannot be very far off when all correction will be impossible; but with that time the period of my real influence will commence, and this period, I trust, will be a long one, for I firmly rely upon Seneca's promise: "*Etiamsi omnibus tecum viventibus silentium livor indixerit; venient qui sine offensa, sine gratia judicent.*" [1] I have done what I could, therefore, to improve this work of my youth, and, considering the brevity and uncertainty of life, I must even regard it as an especially fortunate circumstance, to have been thus permitted to correct in my sixtieth year what I had written in my twenty-sixth.

Nevertheless, while doing this, I meant to deal leniently with my younger self, and to let him discourse, nay, even speak his mind freely, wherever it was possible. But

[1] Seneca, Ep. 79.

ix

wherever he had advanced what was incorrect or superfluous, or had even left out the best part, I have been
obliged to interrupt the thread of his discourse.   And
this has happened often enough ; so often, indeed, that
some of my readers may perhaps think they hear an old
man reading a young man's book aloud, while he frequently
lets it drop, in order to indulge in digressions of his own
on the same subject.

It is easy to see that a work thus corrected after so long
an interval, could never acquire the unity and rounded
completeness which only belong to such as are written in
one breath. So great a difference will be found even in style
and expression, that no reader of any tact can ever be in
doubt whether it be the older or younger man who is speaking. For the contrast is indeed striking between the mild,
unassuming tone in which the youth—who is still simple
enough to believe quite seriously that for all whose pur-
suit is philosophy, truth, and truth alone, can have importance, and therefore that whoever promotes truth is
sure of a welcome from them—propounds his arguments
with confidence, and the firm, but also at times somewhat
harsh voice of the old man, who in course of time has
necessarily discovered the true character and real aims of
the noble company of mercenary time-servers into which
he has fallen. Nay, the just reader will hardly find fault
with him should he occasionally give free vent to his
indignation; since we see what comes of it when people
who profess to have truth for their sole aim, are always
occupied in studying the purposes of their powerful
superiors, and when the *e quovis ligno fit Mercurius* is
extended even to the greatest philosophers, and a clumsy
charlatan, like Hegel, is calmly classed among them ?
Verily German Philosophy stands before us loaded with
contempt, the laughing-stock of other nations, expelled
from all honest science—like the prostitute who sells her-

self for sordid hire to-day to one, to-morrow to another; and the brains of the present generation of *savants* are disorganised by Hegelian nonsense: incapable of reflection, coarse and bewildered, they fall a prey to the low Materialism which has crept out of the basilisk's egg. Good speed to them. I return to my subject.

My readers will thus have to get over the difference of tone in this treatise; for I could not do here what I had done in my chief work, that is, give the later additions I had made in a separate appendix. Besides, it is of no consequence that people should know what I wrote in my twenty-sixth and what in my sixtieth year; the only matter of real importance is, that those who wish to find their way through the fundamental principles of all philosophizing, to gain a firm footing and a clear insight, should in these few sheets receive a little volume by which they may learn something substantial, solid, and true: and this, I hope, will be the case. From the expansion now given to some portions, it has even grown into a compendious theory of the entire faculty of knowing, and this theory, by limiting itself strictly to the research of the Principle of Sufficient Reason, shows the matter from a new and peculiar side; but then it finds its completion in the First Book of " The World as Will and Representation," together with those chapters of the Second Volume which refer to it, and also in my Critique of Kantian Philosophy.

ARTHUR SCHOPENHAUER

FRANKFURT AM MAIN,
       September, 1847.

ON THE FOURFOLD ROOT

OF THE

PRINCIPLE OF SUFFICIENT REASON.

CHAPTER I.

INTRODUCTION.

§ 1. *The Method.*

THE divine Plato and the marvellous Kant unite their mighty voices in recommending a rule, to serve as the method of all philosophising as well as of all other science.[1] Two laws, they tell us: the law of *homogeneity* and the law of *specification*, should be equally observed, neither to the disadvantage of the other. The law of *homogeneity* directs us to collect things together into kinds, by observing their resemblances and correspondences, to collect kinds again into species, species into genera, and so on, till at last we come to the highest all-comprehensive conception. Now this law, being transcendental, *i.e.* essential to our Reason, takes for granted that Nature conforms with it: an assumption which is expressed by the ancient formula, *entia præter necessitatem non esse multi-*

---

[1] Platon, "Phileb." pp. 219-223. "Politic." 62, 63. "Phædr." 361-363, ed. Bip. Kant, "Kritik der reinen Vernunft. Anhang zur transcend. Dialektik." English Translation by F. Max Müller. "Appendix to the Transc. Dialectic." pp. 551, and *seqq.*

plicanda. As for the law of *specification,* Kant expresses
it thus: *entium varietates non temere esse minuendas.* It
requires namely, that we should clearly distinguish one
from another the different genera collected under one comprehensive conception; likewise that we should not confound the higher and lower species comprised in each
genus; that we should be careful not to overleap any, and
never to classify inferior species, let alone individuals,
immediately under the generic conception: each conception being susceptible of subdivision, and none even
coming down to mere intuition. Kant teaches that both
laws are transcendental, fundamental principles of our
Reason, which postulate conformity of things with them
à priori; and Plato, when he tells us that these rules
were flung down from the seat of the gods with the Pro-
methean fire, seems to express the same thought in his
own way.

§ 2. *Application of the Method in the present case.*

In spite of the weight of such recommendations, I find
that the second of these two laws has been far too rarely
applied to a fundamental principle of all knowledge: *the
Principle of Sufficient Reason.* For although this principle
has been often and long ago stated in a general way, still
sufficient distinction has not been made between its extremely different applications, in each of which it acquires
a new meaning; its origin in various mental faculties thus
becoming evident. If we compare Kant's philosophy with
all preceding systems, we perceive that, precisely in the
observation of our mental faculties, many persistent errors
have been caused by applying the principle of homogeneity,
while the opposite principle of specification was neglected;
whereas the law of specification has led to the greatest and
most important results. I therefore crave permission to

quote a passage from Kant, in which the application of the law of specification to the sources of our knowledge is especially recommended; for it gives countenance to my present endeavour:—

"It is of the highest importance to *isolate* various sorts of knowledge, which in kind and origin are different from others, and to take great care lest they be mixed up with those others with which, for practical purposes, they are generally united. What is done by the chemist in the analysis of substances, and by the mathematician in pure mathematics, is far more incumbent on the philosopher, in order to enable him to define clearly the part which, in the promiscuous employment of the understanding, belongs to a special kind of knowledge, as well as its peculiar value and influence." [1]

§ 3. *Utility of this Inquiry.*

Should I succeed in showing that the principle which forms the subject of the present inquiry does not issue directly from *one* primitive notion of our intellect, but rather in the first instance from *various* ones, it will then follow, that neither can the necessity it brings with it, as a firmly established *à priori* principle, be *one* and the *same* in all cases, but must, on the contrary, be as manifold as the sources of the principle itself. Whoever therefore bases a conclusion upon this principle, incurs the obligation of clearly specifying on which of its grounds of necessity he founds his conclusion and of designating that ground by a special name, such as I am about to suggest. I hope that this may be a step towards promoting greater lucidity and precision in philosophising; for I hold the extreme

---

[1] Kant, "Krit. d. r. V. Methodenlehre. Drittes Hauptstück," p. 842 of the 1st edition. Engl. Tr. by F. M. Müller. "Architectonic of Pure Reason," p. 723.

clearness to be attained by an accurate definition of each
single expression to be indispensable to us, as a defence
both against error and against intentional deception, and
also as a means of securing to ourselves the permanent,
unalienable possession of each newly acquired notion within
the sphere of philosophy beyond the fear of losing it
again on account of any misunderstanding or double
meaning which might hereafter be detected. The true
philosopher will indeed always seek after light and perspi-
cuity, and will endeavour to resemble a Swiss lake—which
through its peacefulness is enabled to unite great depth
with great clearness, the depth revealing itself precisely
by the clearness—rather than a turbid, impetuous moun-
tain torrent. "*La clarté est la bonne foi des philosophes,*"
says Vauvenargues. Pseudo-philosophers, on the contrary, use speech, not indeed to conceal their thoughts,
as M. de Talleyrand has it, but rather to conceal the
absence of them, and are apt to make their readers
responsible for the incomprehensibility of their systems,
which really proceeds from their own confused thinking.
This explains why in certain writers—Schelling, for instance
—the tone of instruction so often passes into that of re-
proach, and frequently the reader is even taken to task
beforehand for his assumed inability to understand.

§ 4. *Importance of the Principle of Sufficient Reason.*

Its importance is indeed very great, since it may truly
be called the basis of all science. For by *science* we understand a *system* of notions, *i.e.* a totality of connected,
as opposed to a mere aggregate of disconnected, notions.
But what is it that binds together the members of a system,
if not the Principle of Sufficient Reason? That which
distinguishes every science from a mere aggregate is precisely, that its notions are derived one from another as from

their reason. So it was long ago observed by Plato: καὶ γὰρ αἱ δόξαι αἱ ἀληθεῖς οὐ πολλοῦ ἄξιαί εἰσιν, ἕως ἄν τις αὐτὰς δήσῃ αἰτίας λογισμῷ (*etiam opiniones veræ non multi pretii sunt, donec quis illas ratiocinatione a causis ducta liget*).[1] Nearly every science, moreover, contains notions of causes from which the effects may be deduced, and likewise other notions of the necessity of conclusions from reasons, as will be seen during the course of this inquiry. Aristotle has expressed this as follows: πᾶσα ἐπιστήμη διανοητική, ἢ καὶ μετέχουσά τι διανοίας, περὶ αἰτίας καὶ ἀρχὰς ἐστι (*omnis intellectualis scientia, sive aliquo modo intellectu participans, circa causas et principia est*).[2] Now, as it is this very assumption *à priori* that all things must have their reason, which authorizes us everywhere to search for the *why*, we may safely call this *why* the mother of all science.

§ 5. *The Principle itself.*

We purpose showing further on that the Principle of Sufficient Reason is an expression common to several *à priori* notions. Meanwhile, it must be stated under some formula or other. I choose Wolf's as being the most comprehensive : *Nihil est sine ratione cur potius sit, quam non sit.* Nothing is without a reason for its being.[3]

[1] "Meno." p. 385, ed Bip. "Even true opinions are not of much value until somebody binds them down by proof of a cause." [Translator's addition.]

[2] Aristot. "Metaph." v. 1. "All knowledge which is intellectual or partakes somewhat of intellect, deals with causes and principles." [Tr.'s add.]

[3] Here the translator gives Schopenhauer's free version of Wolf's formula

CHAPTER II.

§ 6. *First Statement of the Principle and Distinction between Two of its Meanings.*

A MORE or less accurately defined, abstract expression for so fundamental a principle of all knowledge must have been found at a very early age; it would, therefore, be difficult, and besides of no great interest, to determine where it first appeared. Neither Plato nor Aristotle have formally stated it as a leading fundamental principle, although both often speak of it as a self-evident truth. Thus, with a *naïveté* which savours of the state of innocence as opposed to that of the knowledge of good and of evil, when compared with the critical researches of our own times, Plato says: ἀναγκαῖον, πάντα τὰ γιγνόμενα διά τινα αἰτίαν γίγνεσθαι· πῶς γὰρ ἂν χωρὶς τούτων γίγνοιτο ; [1] (*necesse est, quæcunque fiunt, per aliquam causum fieri: quomodo enim absque ea fierent ?*) and then again: πᾶν δὲ τὸ γιγνόμενον ὑπ᾽ αἰτίου τινὸς ἐξ ἀνάγκης γίγνεσθαι· παντὶ γὰρ ἀδύνατον χωρὶς αἰτίου γένεσιν σχεῖν [2] (*quidquid gignitur, ex aliqua causa*

---

[1] Platon, "Phileb." p. 240, ed Bip. " It is necessary that all which arises, should arise by some cause; for how could it arise otherwise ? " [Tr.'s add.]

[2] *Ibid.* "Timæus," p. 302. " All that arises, arises necessarily from some cause; for it is impossible for anything to come into being without cause." [Tr.'s add.]

*necessario gignitur: sine causa enim oriri quidquam, im-
possibile est*). At the end of his book " De fato," Plutarch
cites the following among the chief propositions of the
Stoics : μάλιστα μὲν καὶ πρῶτον εἶναι δόξειε, τὸ μηδὲν ἀναιτίως
γίγνεσθαι, ἀλλὰ κατὰ προηγουμένας αἰτίας¹ (*maxime id primum
esse videbitur, nihil fieri sine causa, sed omnia causis ante-
gressis*).

In the "Analyt. post." i. 2, Aristotle states the principle
of sufficient reason to a certain degree when he says :
ἐπίστασθαι δὲ οἰόμεθα ἕκαστον ἁπλῶς, ὅταν τὴν τ᾽ αἰτίαν
οἰόμεθα γινώσκειν, δι᾽ ἣν τὸ πρᾶγμα ἔστιν, ὅτι ἐκείνου αἰτία ἐστίν,
καὶ μὴ ἐνδέχεσθαι τοῦτο ἄλλως εἶναι. (*Scire autem putamus
unamquamque rem simpliciter, quum putamus causam cog-
noscere, propter quum res est, ejusque rei causam esse, nec posse
eam aliter se habere.*)² In his " Metaphysics," moreover,
he already divides causes, or rather principles, ἀρχαί, into
different kinds,³ of which he admits eight ; but this division
is neither profound nor precise enough. He is, nevertheless,
quite right in saying, πασῶν μὲν οὖν κοινὸν τῶν ἀρχῶν, τὸ
πρῶτον εἶναι, ὅθεν ἢ ἔστιν, ἢ γίνεται, ἢ γιγνώσκεται.⁴ (*Omnibus
igitur principiis commune est, esse primum, unde aut est, aut
fit, aut cognoscitur.*) In the following chapter he distinguishes several kinds of causes, although somewhat superficially and confusedly. In the "Analyt. post." ii. 11, he
states four kinds of causes in a more satisfactory manner :

¹ " This especially would seem to be the first principle : that nothing
arises without cause, but [everything] according to preceding causes."
[Tr.'s add.]

² " We think we understand a thing perfectly, whenever we think we
know the cause by which the thing is, that it is really the cause of
that thing, and that the thing cannot possibly be otherwise." [Tr.'s
add.]

³ Lib. iv. c. 1.

⁴ " Now it is common to all principles, that they are the first thing
through which [anything] is, or arises, or is understood." [Tr.'s
add.]

αἰτίαι δὲ τέσσαρες· μία μὲν τό τι ἦν εἶναι· μία δὲ τὸ τινῶν ὄντων, ἀνάγκη τοῦτο εἶναι· ἑτέρα δὲ, ἤ τι πρῶτον ἐκίνησε· τετάρτη δὲ, τὸ τίνος ἕνεκα.[1] (*Causæ autem quatuor sunt : una quæ explicat quid res sit ; altera, quam, si quædam sint, necesse est esse ; tertia, quæ quid primum movit ; quarta id, cujus gratia.*) Now this is the origin of the division of the *causæ* universally adopted by the Scholastic Philosophers, into *causæ materiales, formales, efficientes et finales*, as may be seen in " Suarii disputationes metaphysicæ " [2]—a real compendium of Scholasticism. Even Hobbes still quotes and explains this division.[3] It is also to be found in another passage of Aristotle, this time somewhat more clearly and fully developed (" Metaph." i. 3.) and it is again briefly noticed in the book " De somno et vigilia," c. 2. As for the vitally important distinction between *reason* and *cause*, however, Aristotle no doubt betrays something like a conception of it in the "Analyt. post." i. 13, where he shows at considerable length that knowing and proving *that* a thing exists is a very different thing from knowing and proving *why* it exists : what he represents as the latter, being knowledge of the *cause ;* as the former, knowledge of the *reason*. If, however, he had quite clearly recognized the difference between them, he would never have lost sight of it, but would have adhered to it throughout his writings. Now this is not the case ; for even when he endeavours to distinguish the various kinds of causes from one another, as in the passages I have mentioned above, the essential difference mooted in the chapter just alluded to, never seems to occur to him again. Besides he uses the term αἴτιον indiscriminately for every kind of cause, often indeed calling reasons of know-

---

[1] " There are four causes : first, the essence of a thing itself ; second, the *sine qua non* of a thing ; third, what first put a thing in motion ; fourth, to what purpose or end a thing is tending." [Tr.'s add.]

[2] " Suarii disputationes metaph." Disp. 12, sect. 2 et 3.

[3] Hobbes, " De corpore," P. ii. c. 10, § 7.

ledge, and sometimes even the premisses of a conclusion, αἰτίας, as, for instance, in his "Metaph." iv. 18; "Rhet." ii. 2; "De plantis," i. p. 816 (ed. Berol.), but more especially "Analyt. post." i. 2, where he calls the premisses to a conclusion simply αἰτίαι τοῦ συμπεράσματος (causes of the conclusion). Now, using the same word to express two closely connected conceptions, is a sure sign that their difference has not been recognised, or at any rate not been firmly grasped; for a mere accidental homonymous designation of two widely differing things is quite another matter. Nowhere, however, does this error appear more conspicuously than in his definition of the sophism non causæ ut causa, παρὰ τὸ μὴ αἴτιον ὡς αἴτιον (reasoning from what is not cause as if it were cause), in the book "De sophisticis elenchis," c. 5. By αἴτιον he here understands absolutely nothing but the argument, the premisses, consequently a reason of knowledge; for this sophism consists in correctly proving the impossibility of something, while the proof has no bearing whatever upon the proposition in dispute, which it is nevertheless supposed to refute. Here, therefore, there is no question at all of physical causes. Still the use of the word αἴτιον has had so much weight with modern logicians, that they hold to it exclusively in their accounts of the fallacia extra dictionem, and explain the fallacia non causæ ut causa as designating a physical cause, which is not the case. Reimarus, for instance, does so, and G. E. Schultze and Fries—all indeed of whom I have any knowledge. The first work in which I find a correct definition of this sophism, is Twesten's Logic. Moreover, in all other scientific works and controversies the charge of a fallacia non causæ ut causa usually denotes the interpolation of a wrong cause.

Sextus Empiricus presents another forcible instance of the way in which the Ancients were wont universally to confound the logical law of the reason of knowledge with the transcendental law of cause and effect in Nature, persistently mistaking one for the other. In the 9th Book "Adversus Mathematicos," that is, the Book "Adversus Physicos," § 204, he undertakes to prove the law of causality, and says : "He who asserts that there is no cause (αἰτία), either has no cause (αἰτία) for his assertion, or has one. In the former case there is not more truth in his assertion than in its contradiction ; in the latter, his assertion itself proves the existence of a cause."

By this we see that the Ancients had not yet arrived at a clear distinction between requiring a reason as the ground of a conclusion, and asking for a cause for the occurrence of a real event. As for the Scholastic Philosophers of later times, the law of causality was in their eyes an axiom above investigation: "*non inquirimus an causa sit, quia nihil est per se notius*," says Suarez.[1] At the same time they held fast to the above quoted Aristotelian classification ; but, as far as I know at least, they equally failed to arrive at a clear idea of the necessary distinction of which we are here speaking.

§ 7. *Descartes.*

For we find even the excellent Descartes, who gave the first impulse to subjective reflection and thereby became the father of modern philosophy, still entangled in confusions for which it is difficult to account; and we shall soon see to what serious and deplorable consequences these confusions have led with regard to Metaphysics. In the "*Responsio ad secundas objectiones in meditationes de prima philosophia*," axioma i. he says : *Nulla res existit, de qua non possit quæri, quænam sit causa, cur existat. Hoc enim de ipso Deo quæri potest, non quod indigeat ulla causa ut existat,*

---

[1] Suarez, "Disp." 12, sect. 1.

sea quia ipsa ejus naturæ immensitas est CAUSA, SIVE RATIO,. *propter quam nulla causa indiget ad existendum.* He ought to have said: The immensity of God is a logical reason from which it follows, that God needs no cause; whereas he confounds the two together and obviously has no clear consciousness of the difference between reason and cause. Properly speaking however, it is his intention which mars his insight. For here, where the law of causality demands a *cause*, he substitutes a *reason* instead of it, because the latter, unlike the former, does not immediately lead to something beyond it; and thus, by means of this very axiom, he clears the way to the *Ontological Proof* of the existence of God, which was really his invention, for Anselm had only indicated it in a general manner. Immediately after these axioms, of which I have just quoted the first, there comes a formal, quite serious statement of the Onto-logical Proof, which, in fact, already lies within that axiom, as the chicken does within the egg that has been long brooded over. Thus, while everything else stands in need of a cause for its existence, the *immensitas* implied in the conception of the Deity—who is introduced to us upon the ladder of the Cosmological Proof—suffices in lieu of a cause or, as the proof itself expresses it: *in conceptu entis summe perfecti existentia necessaria continetur.* This, then, is the sleight-of-hand trick, for the sake of which the confusion, familiar even to Aristotle, of the two principal meanings of the principle of sufficient reason, has been used directly *in majorem Dei gloriam.*

Considered by daylight, however, and without prejudice,. this famous Ontological Proof is really a charming joke.. On some occasion or other, some one excogitates a conception, composed out of all sorts of predicates, among which however he takes care to include the predicate actuality or existence, either openly stated or wrapped up for decency's sake in some other predicate, such as *perfectio, immensitas,* or something of the kind.   Now, it is well known,—that, from a given conception, those predicates which are essential to it—*i.e.*, without which it cannot be thought—and likewise the predicates which are essential to those predicates themselves, may be extracted by means of purely logical analyses, and consequently have *logical* truth : that is, they have their reason of knowledge in the given conception. Accordingly the predicate reality or existence is now extracted from this arbitrarily thought conception, and an object corresponding to it is forthwith presumed to have real existence independently of the conception.

> " Wär' der Gedank' nicht so verwünscht gescheut,
> Man wär' versucht ihn herzlich dumm zu nennen." [1]

After all, the simplest answer to such ontological demonstrations is : " All depends upon the source whence you have derived your conception : if it be taken from experience, all well and good, for in this case its object exists and needs no further proof ; if, on the contrary, it has been hatched in your own *sinciput*, all its predicates are of no avail, for it is a mere phantasm.   But we form an unfavourable prejudice against the pretensions of a theology which needed to have recourse to such proofs as this in order to gain a footing on the territory of philosophy, to which it is quite foreign, but on which it longs to trespass.   But oh! for the prophetic wisdom of Aristotle !   He had never even heard of the Ontological Proof ; yet as though he could detect this piece of scholastic jugglery through the shades of coming darkness and were anxious to bar the road to it, he carefully shows [2] that defining a thing and proving its existence are two different matters, separate to all eternity ;

[1]   " Were not the thought so cursedly acute,
         One might be tempted to declare it silly."
     SCHILLER, " Wallenstein-Trilogie. Piccolomini," Act ii. Sc. 7.

[2] Aristot., " Analyt. post." c. 7.

since by the one we learn *what* it is that is meant, and by the other *that* such a thing exists. Like an oracle of the future, he pronounces the sentence : τὸ δ᾽ εἶναι οὐκ οὐσία οὐδενί· οὐ γὰρ γένος τὸ ὄν : (ESSE *autem nullius rei essentia est, quandoquidem ens non est genus*) which means : " Existence never can belong to the essence of a thing." On the other hand, we may see how great was Herr von Schelling's veneration for the Ontological Proof in a long note, p. 152, of the 1st vol. of his "Philosophische Schriften" of 1809. We may even see in it something still more instructive, *i.e.*, how easily Germans allow sand to be thrown in their eyes by impudence and blustering swagger. But for so thoroughly pitiable a creature as Hegel, whose whole pseudo-philosophy is but a monstrous amplification of the Ontological Proof, to have undertaken its defence against Kant, is indeed an alliance of which the Ontological Proof itself might be ashamed, however little it may in general be given to blushing. How can I be expected to speak with deference of men, who have brought philosophy into contempt ?

§ 8. *Spinoza.*

Although Spinoza's philosophy mainly consists in the negation of the double dualism between God and the world and between soul and body, which his teacher, Descartes, had set up, he nevertheless remained true to his master in confounding and interchanging the relation between reason and consequence with that between cause and effect ; he even endeavoured to draw from it a still greater advantage for his own metaphysics than Descartes for his, for he made this confusion the foundation of his whole Pantheism.

A conception contains *implicite* all its essential predicates, so that they may be developed out of it *explicite* by means of mere analytical judgments : the sum total of

them being its definition. This definition therefore differs
from the conception itself merely in form and not in content; for it consists of judgments which are all contained within that conception, and therefore have their
reason in it, in as far as they show its essence. We may
accordingly look upon these judgments as the consequences of that conception, considered as their reason.
Now this relation between a conception and the judgments founded upon it and susceptible of being developed
out of it by analysis, is precisely the relation between
Spinoza's so-called God and the world, or rather between
the one and only substance and its numberless accidents
(*Deus, sive substantia constans infinitis attributis* [1]—*Deus,
sive omnia Dei attributa*). It is therefore the relation in
knowledge of the *reason* to its consequent; whereas true
Theism (Spinoza's Theism is merely nominal) assumes
the relation of the *cause* to its effect, in which the cause
remains different and separate from the consequence, not
only in the way in which we consider them, but really and
essentially, therefore in themselves to all eternity. For
the word God, honestly used, means a cause such as this
of the world, with the addition of personality. An imper-
sonal God is, on the contrary, a *contradictio in adjecto*.
Now as nevertheless, even in the case as stated by him,
Spinoza desired to retain the word God to express substance, and explicitly called this the *cause* of the world, he
could find no other way to do it than by completely inter-
mingling the two relations, and confounding the principle
of the reason of knowledge with the principle of causality.
I call attention to the following passages in corroboration
of this statement. *Notandum, dari necessario unius cujus-
que rei existentis certam aliquam* CAUSAM, *propter quam
existit. Et notandum, hanc causam, propter quam aliqua res
existit, vel debere contineri in ipsa natura et* DEFINITIONE

[1] Spinoza, " Eth." i. prop. 11.

rei existentis (*nimirum quod ad ipsius naturam pertinet existere*), *vel debere* EXTRA *ipsam dari.*[1] In the last case he means an efficient cause, as appears from what follows, whereas in the first he means a mere reason of knowledge; yet he identifies both, and by this means prepares the way for identifying God with the world, which is his intention. This is the artifice of which he always makes use, and which he has learnt from Descartes. He substitutes a cause acting from without, for a reason of knowledge lying within, a given conception. *Ex necessitate divinæ naturæ omnia, quæ sub intellectum infinitum cadere possunt, sequi debent.*[2] At the same time he calls God everywhere the cause of the world. *Quidquid existit Dei potentiam, quæ omnium rerum* CAUSA *est, exprimit.*[3]—*Deus est omnium rerum* CAUSA *immanens, non vero transiens.*[4]— *Deus non tantam est* CAUSA EFFICIENS *rerum existentiæ, sed etiam essentiæ.*[5]—*Ex data quacunque* IDEA *aliquis* EFFECTUS *necessario sequi debat.*[6]—And: *Nulla res nisi a causa externa potest destrui.*[7]—Demonstr. DEFINITIO *cujuscunque rei, ipsius essentiam* (essence, nature, as differing from *existentia*, existence), *affirmat, sed non negat; sive rei essentiam ponit, sed non tollit. Dum itaque ad rem ipsam tantum, non autem ad causas externas attendimus, nihil in eadem poterimus invenire, quod ipsam possit destruere.* This means, that as no conception can contain anything which contradicts its definition, *i.e.*, the sum total of its predicates, neither can an existence contain anything which might become a cause of its destruction. This view, however, is brought to a climax in the somewhat lengthy second demonstration of the 11th Proposition, in which he confounds a cause capable of destroying or anni-

---

[1] Spinoza, "Eth." P. 1. prop. 8, schol. 2.
[2] *Ibid.* Prop. 16.   [3] *Ibid.* Prop. 36, demonstr.
[4] *Ibid.* Prop. 18.   [5] *Ibid.* Prop. 25.
[6] "Eth." P. iii. prop. 1, demonstr.   [7] *Ibid.* Prop. 4.

hilating a being, with a contradiction contained in its
definition and therefore destroying that definition. His
need of confounding cause with reason here becomes so
urgent, that he can never say *causa* or *ratio* alone, but
always finds it necessary to put *ratio seu causa*. Accordingly, this occurs as many as eight times in the same page,
in order to conceal the subterfuge. Descartes had done
the same in the above-mentioned axiom.

Thus, properly speaking, Spinoza's Pantheism is merely
the *realisation* of Descartes' Ontological Proof. First, he
adopts Descartes' ontotheological proposition, to which we
have alluded above, *ipsa naturæ Dei immensitas est* CAUSA
SIVE RATIO, *propter quam nulla causa indiget ad existendum*, always saying *substantia* instead of *Deus* (in the
beginning); and then he finishes by *substantiæ essentia
necessario involvit existentiam, ergo erit substantia* CAUSA
SUI.[1] Therefore the very same argument which Descartes
had used to prove the existence of God, is used by Spinoza
to prove the existence of the world,—which consequently
needs no God. He does this still more distinctly in the
2nd Scholium to the 8th Proposition: *Quoniam ad naturam substantia pertinet existere, debet ejus definitio necessa-
riam existentiam involvere, et consequenter ex sola ejus
definitione debet ipsius existentia concludi.* But this substance is, as we know, the world. The demonstration to
Proposition 24 says in the same sense: *Id, cujus natura in
se considerata (i.e.,* in its definition) *involvit existentiam, est*
CAUSA SUI.

For what Descartes had stated in an exclusively *ideal*
and *subjective* sense, *i.e.*, only for us, for *cognitive purposes*
—in this instance for the sake of proving the existence of
God—Spinoza took in a *real* and *objective* sense, as the
actual relation of God to the world. According to Descartes, the existence of God is contained in the *conception*

[1] "Eth." P. i. prop. 7.

of God, therefore it becomes an argument for his actual
being: according to Spinoza, God is himself contained
in the world. Thus what, with Descartes, was only
reason of knowledge, becomes, with Spinoza, reason of
fact. If the former, in his Ontological Proof, taught
that the *existentia* of God is a consequence of the *essentia*
of God, the latter turns this into *causa sui*, and boldly
opens his Ethics with : *per causam sui intelligo id, cujus
essentia* (conception) *involvit existentiam*, remaining deaf
to Aristotle's warning cry, τὸ δ᾽ εἶναι οὐκ οὐσία οὐδενί!
Now, this is the most palpable confusion of *reason* and
cause. And if Neo-Spinozans (Schellingites, Hegelians,
&c.), with whom words are wont to pass for thoughts,
often indulge in pompous, solemn admiration for this
causa sui, for my own part I see nothing but a *contradictio in adjecto* in this same *causa sui*, a *before* that is
after, an audacious command to us, to sever arbitrarily the
eternal causal chain—something, in short, very like the
proceeding of that Austrian, who finding himself unable
to reach high enough to fasten the clasp on his tightly-
strapped shako, got upon a chair. The right emblem for
causa sui is Baron Münchhausen, sinking on horseback
into the water, clinging by the legs to his horse and pull-
ing both himself and the animal out by his own pigtail,
with the motto underneath: *Causa sui.*

Let us finally cast a look at the 16th proposition of the
1st book of the Ethics. Here we find Spinoza concluding
from the proposition, *ex data cujuscunque rei definitione
plures proprietates intellectus concludit, quæ revera ex eadem
necessario sequuntur*, that *ex necessitate divinæ naturæ* (*i.e.*,
taken as a reality), *infinita infinitis modis sequi debent* :
this God therefore unquestionably stands in the same
relation to the world as a conception to its definition. The
corollary, *Deum omnium rerum esse* CAUSAM EFFICIENTEM,
is nevertheless immediately connected with it. It is im-

possible to carry the confusion between reason and cause
farther, nor could it lead to graver consequences than here.
But this shows the importance of the subject of the present
treatise.

In endeavouring to add a third step to the climax in
question, Herr von Schelling has contributed a small after-
piece to these errors, into which two mighty intellects of
the past had fallen owing to insufficient clearness in thinking. If Descartes met the demands of the inexorable law of
causality, which reduced his God to the last straits, by substituting a reason instead of the cause required, in order thus
to set the matter at rest; and if Spinoza made a real cause
out of this reason, *i.e.*, *causa sui*, his God thereby becoming
the world itself: Schelling now made reason and consequent
separate in God himself.[1] He thus gave the thing still
greater consistency by elevating it to a real, substantial
hypostasis of reason and consequent, and introducing us
to something " in God, which is not himself, but his
reason, as a primary reason, or rather reason beyond reason
(abyss)." *Hoc quidem vere palmarium est.*—It is now
known that Schelling had taken the whole fable from
Jacob Böhme's " Full account of the terrestrial and celestial mystery; " but what appears to me to be less well
known, is the source from which Jacob Böhme himself
had taken it, and the real birth-place of this so-called
abyss, wherefore I now take the liberty to mention it. It
is the βυθός, i.e. *abyssus, vorago*, bottomless pit, reason
beyond reason of the Valentinians (a heretical sect of the
second century) which, in silence—co-essential with itself
—engendered intelligence and the world, as Irenæus[2] re-
lates in the following terms: λέγουσι γάρ τινα εἶναι ἐν
ἀοράτοις, καὶ ἀκατονομάστοις ὑψώμασι τέλειον Αἰῶνα προόντα·
τοῦτον δὲ καὶ προαρχήν, καὶ προπάτορα, καὶ βυθὸν καλοῦσιν.—

[1] Schelling, " Abhandlung von der mensch'ichen Freiheit."
[2] Irenæus, " Contr. hæres." lib. i. c. 1.

—Ὑπάρχοντα δὲ αὐτὸν ἀχώρητον καὶ ἀόρατον, ἀΐδιόν τε καὶ ἀγέννητον, ἐν ἡσυχίᾳ καὶ ἠρεμίᾳ πολλῇ γεγονέναι ἐν ἀπείροις αἰῶσι χρόνων. Συννπάρχειν δὲ αὐτῷ καὶ Ἔννοιαν, ἣν δὲ καὶ Χάριν, καὶ Σιγὴν ὀνομάζουσι· καὶ ἐννοηθῆναί ποτε ἀφ᾿ ἑαυτοῦ προβαλέσθαι τὸν βυθὸν τοῦτον ἀρχὴν τῶν πάντων, καὶ καθάπερ σπέρμα τὴν προβολὴν ταύτην (ἣν προβαλέσθαι ἐνενοήθη) καθέσθαι, ὡς ἐν μήτρᾳ, τῇ συννπαρχούσῃ, ἑαυτῷ Σιγῇ. Ταύτην δὲ, ὑποδηξαμένην τὸ σπέρμα τοῦτο, καὶ ἐγκύμονα γενομένην, ἀποκυῆσαι Νοῦν, ὅμοιόν τε καὶ ἴσον τῷ προβαλόντι, καὶ μόνον χωροῦντα τὸ μέγεθος τοῦ Πατρός. Τὸν δὲ νοῦν τοῦτον καὶ μονογενῆ καλοῦσι, καὶ ἀρχὴν τῶν πάντων.[1] (*Dicunt enim esse quendam in sublimitatibus illis, quæ nec oculis cerni, nec nominari possunt, perfectum Æonem præexistentem, quem et proarchen, et propatorem, et* Bythum *vocant. Eum autem, quum incomprehensibilis et invisibilis, sempiternus idem et ingenitus esset, infinitis temporum seculis in summa quiete ac tranquillitate fuisse. Unâ etiam cum eo Cogitationem exstitisse, quam et Gratiam et Silentium (Sigen) nuncupant. Hunc porro* Bythum *in animum aliquando induxisse, rerum omnium initium proferre, atque hanc, quam in animum induxerat, productionem, in Sigen (silentium) quæ unâ cum eo erat, non·secus atque in vulvam demisisse. Hanc vero, suscepto hoc semine, prægnantem effectam pepe-*

---

[1] " For they say that in those unseen heights which have no name there is a pre-existing, perfect Æon; this they also call fore-rule, forefather and the depth.—They say, that being incomprehensible and invisible, eternal and unborn, he has existed during endless Æons in the deepest calmness and tranquillity; and that coexisting with him was Thought, which they also call Grace and Silence. This Depth once bethought him to put forth from himself the beginning of all things and to lay that offshoot—which he had resolved to put forth—like a sperm into the coexisting Silence, as it were into a womb. Now this Silence, being thus impregnated and having conceived, gave birth to Intellect, a being which was like and equal to its Creator, and alone able to comprehend the greatness of its father. This Intellect also they call the Only-begotten and the Beginning of all things." [Tr.'s add.]

risse Intellectum, parenti suo parem et æqualem, atque ita comparatum, ut solus paternæ magnitudinis capax esset. Atque hunc Intellectum et Monogenem et Patrem et principum omnium rerum appellant.)

Somehow or other this must have come to Jacob Böhme's hearing from the History of Heresy, and Herr von Schelling must have received it from him in all faith.

§ 9. *Leibnitz.*

It was Leibnitz who first formally stated the Principle of Sufficient Reason as a main principle of all knowledge and of all science. He proclaims it very pompously in various passages of his works, giving himself great airs, as though he had been the first to invent it; yet all he finds to say about it is, that everything must have a sufficient reason for being as it is, and not otherwise : and this the world had probably found out before him. True, he makes casual allusions to the distinction between its two chief significations, without, however, laying any particular stress upon it, or explaining it clearly anywhere else. The principal reference to it is in his " Principia Philosophiæ," § 32, and a little more satisfactorily in the French version, entitled " Monadologie " : *En vertu du principe de la raison suffisante, nous considérons qu'aucun fait ne sauroit se trouver vrai ou existant, aucune énonciation véritable, sans qu'il y ait une raison suffisante, pourquoi il en soit ainsi et non pas autrement.*[1]

§ 10. *Wolf.*

The first writer who explicitly separated the two chief significations of our principle, and stated the difference between them in detail, was therefore Wolf. Wolf, how-

---

[1] Compare with this § 44 of his " Theodicée," and his 5th letter to Clarke, § 125.

·ever, does not place the principle of sufficient reason in Logic, as is now the custom, but in Ontology. True, in § 71 he urges the necessity of not confounding the principle ·of sufficient reason of knowing with that of cause and effect; .still he does not clearly determine here where in the difference ·consists. Indeed, he himself mistakes the one for the other; for he quotes instances of cause and effect in confirmation ·of the *principium rationis sufficientis* in this very chapter, *de ratione sufficiente*, §§ 70, 74, 75, 77, which, had he really wished to preserve that distinction, ought rather to have been quoted in the chapter *de causis* of the same work. In said chapter he again brings forward precisely similar instances, and once more enunciates the *principium cogno-scendi* (§ 876), which does not certainly belong to it, having been already discussed, yet which serves to introduce the im-mediately following clear and definite distinction between this principle and the law of causality, §§ 881-884. *Principium*, he continues, *dicitur id, quod in se continet rationem alterius;* and he distinguishes *three* kinds: 1. PRINCIPIUM FIENDI *(causa)*, which he defines as *ratio actualitatis alterius*, e.g., *si lapis calescit, ignis aut radii solares sunt rationes, cur calor lapidi insit.*—2. PRINCIPIUM ESSENDI, which he defines as *ratio possibilitatis alterius; in eodem exemplo, ratio possibilitatis, cur lapis calorem recipere possit, est in essentia seu modo compositionis lapidis.* This last con-ception seems to me inadmissible. If it has any mean-ing at all, possibility means correspondence with the general conditions of experience known to us *à priori*, as Kant has sufficiently shown. From these conditions we know, with respect to Wolf's instance of the stone, that ·changes are possible as effects proceeding from causes : we know, that is, that one state can succeed another, if the former contains the conditions for the latter. In this case we find, as effect, the state of being warm in the stone; .as cause, the preceding state of a limited capacity for warmth in the stone and its contact with free heat. Now, Wolf's naming the first mentioned property of this state *principium essendi*, and the second, *principium fiendi*, rests upon a delusion caused by the fact that, so far as the stone is concerned, the conditions are more lasting and can therefore wait longer for the others. That the stone should be as it is: that is, that it should be chemically so constituted as to bring with it a particular degree of specific heat, consequently a capacity for heat which stands in inverse proportion to its specific heat; that besides it should, on the other hand, come into contact with free heat, is the consequence of a whole chain of antecedent causes, all of them *principia fiendi ;* but it is the coincidence of circumstances on both sides which primarily constitutes that condition, upon which, as cause, the becoming warm depends, as effect. All this leaves no room for Wolf's *principium essendi*, which I therefore do not admit, and concerning which I have here entered somewhat into detail, partly because I mean to use the word myself later on in a totally different sense; partly also, because this explanation contributes to facilitate the comprehension of the law of causality.—3. Wolf, as we have said, distinguishes a PRINCIPIUM COGNOSCENDI, and refers also under *causa* to a *causa impulsiva, sive ratio voluntatem determinans.*

§ 11. *Philosophers between Wolf and Kant.*

Baumgarten repeats the Wolfian distinctions in his "Metaphysica," §§ 20-24, and §§ 306-313.

Reimarus, in his "Vernunftlehre," [1] § 81, distinguishes 1. *Inward reason*, of which his explanation agrees with Wolf's *ratio essendi*, and might even be applicable to the *ratio cognoscendi*, if he did not transfer to things what only applies to conceptions; 2. *Outward reason*, i.e. *causa.*—§ 120

---

[1] Doctrine of Reason.

et seqq., he rightly defines the *ratio cognoscendi* as a condition of the proposition ; but in an example, § 125, he nevertheless confounds it with cause.

Lambert, in the new Organon, does not mention Wolf's distinctions ; he shows, however, that he recognizes a difference between reason of knowledge and cause ;[1] for he says that God is the *principium essendi* of truths, and that truths are the *principia cognoscendi* of God.

Plattner, in his Aphorisms, § 868, says : " What is called reason and conclusion within our knowledge (*principium cognoscendi, ratio—rationatum*), is in reality cause and effect (*causa efficiens—effectus*). Every cause is a reason, every effect a conclusion." He is therefore of opinion that cause and effect, in reality, correspond to the conceptions reason and consequence in our thought ; that the former stand in a similar relation with respect to the latter as substance and accident, for instance, to subject and predicate, or the quality of the object to our sensation of that quality, &c. &c. I think it useless to refute this opinion, for it is easy to see that premisses and conclusion in judgments stand in an entirely different relation to one another from a knowledge of cause and effect ; although in individual cases even knowledge of a cause, as such, may be the reason of a judgment which enunciates the effect.[2]

§ 12. *Hume.*

No one before this serious thinker had ever doubted what follows. First, and before all things in heaven and on earth, is the Principle of Sufficient Reason in the form of the Law of Causality. For it is a *veritas æterna : i.e.* it is in and by itself above Gods and Fate ; whereas everything else, the understanding, for instance, which thinks

---

[1] Lambert, " New Organon," vol. i. § 572.
[2] Compare § 36. of this treatise.

that principle, and no less the whole world and whatever may be its cause—atoms, motion, a Creator, *et cætera*—is what it is only in accordance with, and by virtue of, that principle. Hume was the first to whom it occurred to inquire whence this law of causality derives its authority, and to demand its credentials. Everyone knows the result at which he arrives: that causality is nothing beyond the empirically perceived succession of things and states in Time, with which habit has made us familiar. The fallacy of this result is felt at once, nor is it difficult to refute. The merit lies in the question itself; for it became the impulse and starting-point for Kant's profound researches, and by their means led to an incomparably deeper and more thorough view of Idealism than the one which had hitherto existed, and which was chiefly Berkeley's. It led to transcendental Idealism, from which arises the conviction, that the world is as dependent upon us, as a whole, as we are dependent upon it in detail. For, by pointing out the existence of those transcendental principles, as such, which enable us to determine *à priori, i.e.* before all experience, certain points concerning objects and their possibility, he proved that these things could not exist, as they present themselves to us, independently of our knowledge. The resemblance between a world such as this and a dream, is obvious.

§ 13. *Kant and his School.*

Kant's chief passage on the Principle of Sufficient Reason is in a little work entitled " On a discovery, which is to permit us to dispense with all Criticism of Pure Reason." [1] Section I., *lit.* A. Here he strongly urges the distinction between " the logical (formal) principle of cognition ' every proposition must have its reason,' and the transcen-

---

[1] " Ueber eine Entdeckung, nach der alle Kritik der reinen Vernunft entbehrlich gemacht werden soll."

dental (material) principle 'every thing must have its cause,'" in his controversy with Eberhard, who had identified them as one and the same.—I intend myself to criticize Kant's proof of the à priori and consequently transcendental character of the law of causality further on in a separate paragraph, after having given the only true proof.

With these precedents to guide them, the several writers on Logic belonging to Kant's school; Hofbauer, Maass, Jakob, Kiesewetter and others, have defined pretty accurately the distinction between reason and cause. Kiesewetter, more especially, gives it thus quite satisfactorily: [1] " Reason of knowledge is not to be confounded with reason of fact (cause). The Principle of Sufficient Reason belongs to Logic, that of Causality to Metaphysics.[2] The former is the fundamental principle of thought; the latter that of experience. Cause refers to real things, logical reason has only to do with representations."

Kant's adversaries urge this distinction still more strongly. G. E. Schultze [3] complains that the Principle of Sufficient Reason is confounded with that of Causality. Salomon Maimon [4] regrets that so much should be said about the sufficient reason without an explanation of what is meant by it, while he blames Kant [5] for deriving the principle of causality from the logical form of hypothetical judgments.

F. H. Jacobi [6] says, that by the confounding of the two conceptions, reason and cause, an illusion is produced, which has given rise to various false speculations; and he points out the distinction between them after his own

[1] Kiesewetter, "Logik," vol. i. p. 16.
[2] Ibid. p. 60.
[3] G. E. Schultze, " Logik," § 19, Anmerkung 1, und § 63.
[4] Sal. Maimon, " Logik," p. 20, 21.   [5] Ibid. " Vorrede," p. xxiv.
[6] Jacobi, " Briefe über die Lehre des Spinoza," Beilage 7, p. 414.

fashion. Here, however, as is usual with him, we find a
good deal more of self-complacent phrase-jugglery than of
serious philosophy.

How Herr von Schelling finally distinguishes reason
from cause, may be seen in his "Aphorisms introductory
to the Philosophy of Nature," [1] § 184, which open the first
book of the first volume of Marcus and Schelling's "Annals
of Medecine." Here we are taught that gravity is the
reason and light the *cause* of all things. This I merely
quote as a curiosity; for such random talk would not
otherwise deserve a place among the opinions of serious
and honest inquirers.

§ 14. *On the Proofs of the Principle.*

We have still to record various fruitless attempts which
have been made to prove the Principle of Sufficient Reason,
mostly without clearly defining in which sense it was
taken: Wolf's, for instance, in his Ontology, § 70, repeated
by Baumgarten in his "Metaphysics," § 20. It is useless
to repeat and refute it here, as it obviously rests on a
verbal quibble. Plattner [2] and Jakob [3] have tried other
proofs, in which, however, the circle is easily detected. I
purpose dealing with those of Kant further on, as I have
already said. Since I hope, in the course of this treatise,
to point out the different laws of our cognitive faculties,
of which the principle of sufficient reason is the common
expression, it will result as a matter of course, that this
principle cannot be proved, and that, on the contrary,
Aristotle's remark: [4] λόγον ζητοῦσι ὧν οὐκ ἔστι λόγος.

[1] "Aphorismen zur Einleitung in die Naturphilosophie."
[2] Plattner, "Aphorismen," § 828.
[3] Jakob, "Logik und Metaphysik," p. 38 (1794).
[4] Aristotle, "Metaph." iii. 6. "They seek a reason for that which
has no reason; for the principle of demonstration is not demonstration."
[Tr.'s add.] Compare with this citation "Analyt. post." i. 2.

ἀποδείξεως γὰρ ἀρχὴ οὐκ ἀπόδειξίς ἐστι (*rationem eorum quœrant, quorum non est ratio : demonstrationis enim principium non est demonstratio*) may be applied with equal propriety to all these proofs. For every proof is a reference to something already recognised; and if we continue requiring a proof again for this something, whatever it be, we at last arrive at certain propositions which express the forms and laws, therefore the conditions, of all thought and of all knowledge, in the application of which consequently all thought and all knowledge consists : so that certainty is nothing but correspondence with those conditions, forms, and laws, therefore their own certainty cannot again be ascertained by means of other propositions. In the fifth chapter I mean to discuss the kind of truth which belongs to propositions such as these.

To seek a proof for the Principle of Sufficient Reason, is, moreover, an especially flagrant absurdity, which shows a want of reflection. Every proof is a demonstration of the reason for a judgment which has been pronounced, and which receives the predicate *true* in virtue precisely of that demonstration. This necessity for a reason is exactly what the Principle of Sufficient Reason expresses. Now if we require a proof of it, or, in other words, a demonstration of its reason, we thereby already assume it to be true, nay, we found our demand precisely upon that assumption, and thus we find ourselves involved in the circle of exacting a proof of our right to exact a proof.

CHAPTER III.

§ 15. *Cases which are not comprised among the old established meanings of the Principle.*

FROM the summary given in the preceding chapter we
gather, that two distinct applications of the principle
of sufficient reason have been recognized, although very
gradually, very tardily, and not without frequent relapses
into error and confusion : the one being its application to
judgments, which, to be true, must have a reason; the
other, its application to changes in material objects, which
must always have a cause. In both cases we find the
principle of sufficient reason authorizing us to ask *why?* a
quality which is essential to it. But are all the cases in
which it authorizes us to ask *why* comprised in these two
relations? If I ask: Why are the three sides of this
triangle equal? the answer is : Because the three angles
are so. Now, is the equality of the angles the cause of the
equality of the sides? No; for here we have to do with
no change, consequently with no effect which must have a
cause.—Is it merely a logical reason? No; for the equality
of the angle is not only a proof of the equality of the
sides, it is not only the foundation of a judgment: mere
conceptions alone would never suffice to explain why the
sides must be equal, because the angles are so; for the
conception of the equality of the sides is not contained in
that of the equality of the angles. Here therefore we

have no connection between conceptions and judgments, but between sides and angles. The equality of the angles is not the *direct*, but the *indirect* reason, by which we know the equality of the sides; for it is the reason why a thing is such as it is (in this case, that the sides are equal) : the angles being equal, the sides must therefore be equal. Here we have a necessary connection between angles and sides, not a direct, necessary connection between two judgments.—Or again, if I ask why *infecta facta,* but never *facta infecta fieri possunt,* consequently why the past is absolutely irrevocable, the future inevitable, even this does not admit of purely logical proof by means of mere abstract conceptions, nor does it belong either to causality, which only rules *occurrences* within Time, not Time itself. The present hour hurled the preceding one into the bottomless pit of the past, not through causality, but immediately, through its mere existence, which existence was nevertheless inevitable. It is impossible to make this comprehensible or even clearer by means of mere conceptions; we recognise it, on the contrary, quite directly and instinctively, just as we recognize the difference between right and left and all that depends upon it : for instance, that our left glove will not fit our right hand, &c. &c.

Now, as all those cases in which the principle of sufficient reason finds its application cannot therefore be reduced to logical reason and consequence and to cause and effect, the law of specification cannot have been sufficiently attended to in this classification. The law of homogeneity, however, obliges us to assume, that these cases cannot differ to infinity, but that they may be reduced to certain species. Now, before attempting this classification, it will be necessary to determine what is peculiar to the principle of sufficient reason in all cases, as its special characteristic; because the conception of the genus must always be determined before the conception of the species.

§ 16. *The Roots of the Principle of Sufficient Reason.*

Our knowing consciousness, which manifests itself as outer and inner Sensibility (or receptivity) *and as Understanding and Reason, subdivides itself into Subject and Object and contains nothing else. To be Object for the Subject and to be our representation, are the same thing. All our representations stand towards one another in a regulated connection, which may be determined* À PRIORI, *and on account of which, nothing existing separately and independently, nothing single or detached, can become an Object for us.* It is this connection which is expressed by the Principle of Sufficient Reason in its generality. Now, although, as may be gathered from what has gone before, this connection assumes different forms according to the different kinds of objects, which forms are differently expressed by the Principle of Sufficient Reason; still the connection retains what is common to all these forms, and this is expressed in a general and abstract way by our principle. The relations upon which it is founded, and which will be more closely indicated in this treatise, are what I call the Root of the Principle of Sufficient Reason. Now, on closer inspection, according to the laws of homogeneity and of specification, these relations separate into distinct species, which differ widely from each other. Their number, however, may be reduced to *four*, according to the *four* classes into which everything that can become an object for us—that is to say, all our representations—may be divided. These classes will be stated and considered in the following four chapters.

We shall see the Principle of Sufficient Reason appear under a different form in each of them; but it will also show itself under all as the same principle and as derived from the said root, precisely because it admits of being expressed as above.

CHAPTER IV.

ON THE FIRST CLASS OF OBJECTS FOR THE SUBJECT, AND THAT FORM OF THE PRINCIPLE OF SUFFICIENT REASON WHICH PREDOMINATES IN IT.

§ 17. *General Account of this Class of Objects.*

THE first class of objects possible to our representative faculty, is that of *intuitive, complete, empirical* representations. They are *intuitive* as opposed to mere thoughts, *i.e.* abstract conceptions; they are *complete*, inasmuch as, according to Kant's distinction, they not only contain the formal, but also the material part of phenomena; and they are *empirical*, partly as proceeding, not from a mere connection of thoughts, but from an excitation of feeling in our sensitive organism, as their origin, to which they constantly refer for evidence as to their reality: partly also because they are linked together, according to the united laws of Space, Time and Causality, in that complex without beginning or end which forms our *Empirical Reality*. As, nevertheless, according to the result of Kant's teaching, this *Empirical Reality* does not annul their *Transcendental Ideality*, we shall consider them here, where we have only to do with the formal elements of knowledge, merely as representations.

§ 18. *Outline of a Transcendental Analysis of Empirical Reality.*

The forms of these representations are those of the inner and outer sense; namely, *Time* and *Space*. But these are

only *perceptible* when *filled*. Their *perceptibility* is *Matter,*
to which I shall return further on, and again in § 21. *If
Time were the only form* of these representations, there
could be no *coexistence*, therefore nothing *permanent* and
no *duration*. For *Time* is only perceived when filled, and
its course is only perceived by the *changes* which take place
in that which fills it. The *permanence* of an object is
therefore only recognized by contrast with the *changes* going
on in other objects *coexistent* with it. But the representation of *coexistence* is impossible in Time alone; it depends, for its completion, upon the representation of *Space;*
because, in mere Time, all things *follow one another*, and
in mere Space all things are *side by side;* it is accordingly
only by the combination of Time and Space that the representation of coexistence arises.

On the other hand, were Space the sole form of this class
of representations, there would be no *change;* for change
or alteration is *succession* of states, and *succession* is only
possible in *Time*. We may therefore define Time as the
possibility of opposite states in one and the same thing.

Thus we see, that although infinite divisibility and infinite extension are common to both Time and Space, these
two forms of empirical representations differ fundamentally, inasmuch as what is essential to the *one* is without
any meaning at all for the *other:* juxtaposition having no
meaning in Time, succession no meaning in Space. The
empirical representations which belong to the orderly complex of reality, appear notwithstanding in both forms together; nay, the *intimate union* of both is the condition of
reality which, in a sense, grows out of them, as a product
grows out of its factors. Now it is the Understanding
which, by means of its own peculiar function, brings about
this *union* and connects these heterogeneous forms in such
a manner, that *empirical reality*—albeit only for that
Understanding—arises out of their mutual interpenetra-

tion, and arises as a collective representation, forming a complex, held together by the forms of the principle of sufficient reason, but whose limits are problematical. Each single representation belonging to this class is a part of this complex, each one taking its place in it according to laws known to us *à priori;* in it therefore countless objects *coexist*, because Substance, *i.e.* Matter, remains permanent in spite of the ceaseless flow of Time, and because its states change in spite of the rigid immobility of Space. In this complex, in short, the whole objective, real world exists for us. The reader who may be interested in this, will find the present rough sketch of the analysis of empirical reality further worked out in § 4 of the first volume of "Die Welt als Wille und Vorstellung,"[1] where a closer explanation is given of the way in which the Understanding effects this union and thus creates for itself the empirical world. He will also find a very important help in the table, "*Prædicabilia à priori* of Time, Space, and Matter," which is added to the fourth chapter of the second volume of the same work, and which I recommend to his attention, as it especially shows how the contrasts of Time and Space are equally balanced in Matter, as their product, under the form of Causality.

We shall now proceed to give a detailed exposition of that function of the Understanding which is the basis of empirical reality ; only we must first, by a few incidental explanations, remove the more immediate objections which the fundamental idealism of the view I have adopted might encounter.

[1] Vol. i. p. 12, and *seqq.* of the 1st edition ; p. 9 of the 3rd edition.

§ 19. *Immediate Presence of Representations.*

Now as, notwithstanding this union through the Understanding of the forms of the inner and outer sense in representing Matter and with it a permanent outer world, all
immediate knowledge is nevertheless acquired by the Subject
through the *inner* sense alone—the outer sense being again
Object for the inner, which in its turn perceives the perceptions of the outer—and as therefore, with respect to the
immediate presence of representations in its consciousness,
the Subject remains under the rule of *Time* alone, as the
form of the *inner sense* :[1] it follows, that only one representation can be present to it (the Subject) at the same time,
although that one may be very complicated. When we
speak of representations as *immediately present,* we mean,
that they are not only known in the union of Time and Space
effected by the Understanding—an intuitive faculty, as we
shall soon see—through which the collective representation of empirical reality arises, but that they are known in
mere Time alone, as representations of the inner sense, and
just at the neutral point at which its two currents separate, called the *present.* The necessary condition mentioned in the preceding paragraph for the immediate presence of a representation of this class, is its causal action
upon our senses and consequently upon our organism,
which itself belongs to this class of objects, and is therefore subject to the causal law which predominates in it
and which we are now about to examine. Now as therefore,
on the one hand, according to the laws of the inner and outer
world, the Subject cannot stop short at that one representation; but as, on the other hand, there is no coexistence

---

[1] Compare Kant, "Krit. d. r. Vern." Elementarlehre. Abschnitt ii.
Schlüsse a. d. Begr. *b* and *c.* 1st edition, pp. 33 and 34; 5th edition,
p. 49. (Transl. M. Müller, p. 29, *b* and *c.*)

in Time alone: that single representation must always vanish and be superseded by others, in virtue of a law which we cannot determine à *priori*, but which depends upon circumstances soon to be mentioned. It is moreover a well-known fact, that the imagination and dreams reproduce the immediate presence of representations; the investigation of that fact, however, belongs to empirical Psychology. Now as, notwithstanding the transitory, isolated nature of our representations with respect to their immediate presence in our consciousness, the Subject nevertheless retains the representation of an all-comprehensive complex of reality, as described above, by means of the function of the Understanding; representations have, on the strength of this antithesis, been viewed, as something quite different when considered as belonging to that complex than when considered with reference to their immediate presence in our consciousness. From the former point of view they were called *real things;* from the latter only, representations καr' ἐξοχήν. This view of the matter, which is the ordinary one, is known under the name of *Realism.* On the appearance of modern philosophy, *Idealism* opposed itself to this *Realism* and has since been steadily gaining ground. Malebranche and Berkeley were its earliest representatives, and Kant enhanced it to the power of Transcendental Idealism, by which the co-existence of the Empirical Reality of things with their Transcendental Ideality becomes conceivable, and according to which Kant expresses himself as follows:[1] " *Transcendental Idealism* teaches that all phenomena are representations only, not things by themselves." And again:[2]

[1] Kant, " Krit. d. r. V." Kritik des Vierten Paralogismus der transcendentalen Psychologie, p. 369, 1st edition. (Engl. Transl. by M. Müller, p 320.)

[2] *Ibid.* 1st edition, pp. 374-375. Note. (Engl. Transl. p. 325. Note.)

" Space itself is nothing but mere representation, and whatever is in it must therefore be contained in that representation. There is nothing whatever in Space, except so far
as it is really represented in it." Finally he says : [1] " If we
take away the thinking Subject, the whole material world
must vanish; because it is nothing but a phenomenon in the
sensibility of our own subject and a certain class of its representations." In India, Idealism is even a doctrine of popular
religion, not only of Brahminism, but of Buddhism ; in
Europe alone is it a paradox, in consequence of the essentially and unavoidably realistic principle of Judaism. But
Realism quite overlooks the fact, that the so-called existence of these real things is *absolutely nothing but their
being represented* (*ein Vorgestellt-werden*), or—if it be in-
sisted, that only the immediate presence in the consciousness of the Subject can be called being represented κατ'
ἐντελέχειαν—it is even only a possibility of being represented
κατὰ δύναμιν. The realist forgets that the Object ceases to
be Object apart from its reference to the Subject, and that
if we take away that reference, or think it away, we at
once do away with all objective existence. Leibnitz, while
he clearly felt the Subject to be the necessary condition for
the Object, was nevertheless unable to get rid of the
thought that objects exist by themselves and independently
of all reference whatsoever to the Subject, *i.e.* independently of being represented. He therefore assumed in the
first place a world of objects exactly like the world of
representations and running parallel with it, having no
direct, but only an outward connection with it by means
of a *harmonia præstabilita ;*—obviously the most superfluous thing possible, for it never comes within perception,
and the precisely similar world of representations which
does come within perception, goes its own way regardless

[1] Kant, "Krit. d. r. V." "Betrachtung über die Summe," &c., p. 383
of 1st edition. (Engl. Transl. p. 331.)

of it. When, however, he wanted to determine more closely the essence of these things existing objectively in themselves, he found himself obliged to declare the Objects in themselves to be Subjects (*monades*), and by doing so he furnished the most striking proof of the inability of our consciousness, in as far as it is merely cognitive, to find within the limits of the intellect—*i.e.* of the apparatus by means of which we represent the world—anything beyond Subject and Object; the representer and the represented. Therefore, if we abstract from the objectivity of an Object, or in other words, from its being represented (*Vorgestellt-werden*), if we annul it in its quality as an Object, yet still wish to retain something, we can meet with nothing but *the Subject*. Conversely, if we desire to abstract from the subjectivity of the Subject, yet to have something over, the contrary takes place, and this leads to Materialism.

Spinoza, who never thoroughly sifted the matter, and never therefore acquired a clear notion of it, nevertheless quite understood the necessary correlation between Subject and Object as so essential, that they are inconceivable without it; consequently he defined it as an identity in the Substance (which alone exists) of that which knows, with that which has extension.

OBSERVATION.—With reference to the chief argument of this paragraph, I take the opportunity to remark that if, in the course of this treatise, for the sake of brevity and in order to be more easily understood, I at any time use the term *real objects*, I mean by it nothing but the intuitive representations that are united to form the complex of empirical reality, which reality in itself always remains ideal.

§ 20. *Principle of Sufficient Reason of Becoming.*

In the Class of Objects for the Subject just described, the principle of sufficient reason figures as the *Law of Causality*, and, as such, I call it the *Principle of Sufficient Reason of Becoming, principium rationis sufficientis fiendi.* By it,

all objects presenting themselves within the entire range
of our representation are linked together, as far as the
appearance and disappearance of their states is concerned,
i.e. in the movement of the current of Time, to form the
complex of empirical reality. The law of causality is as
follows. When one or several real objects pass into any
new state, some other state must have preceded this one,
upon which the new state regularly follows, *i.e.* as often as
that preceding one occurs. This sort of following we call
resulting; the first of the states being named a *cause*, the
second an *effect*. When a substance takes fire, for instance,
this state of ignition must have been preceded by a state,
1°, of affinity to oxygen; 2°, of contact with oxygen;
3°, of a given temperature. Now, as ignition must necessarily follow immediately upon this state, and as it has
only just taken place, that state cannot always have been
there, but must, on the contrary, have only just supervened.
This supervening is called a *change*. It is on this account
that the law of causality stands in exclusive relation to
changes and has to do with them alone. Every effect, at the
time it takes place, is a *change* and, precisely by not having
occurred sooner, infallibly indicates some other *change* by
which it has been preceded. That other *change* takes the
name of *cause*, when referred to the following one—of
effect, when referred to a third necessarily preceding *change*.
This is the chain of causality. It is necessarily without a
beginning. By it, each supervening state must have resulted from a preceding change: in the case just mentioned, for instance, from the substance being brought into
contact with free heat, from which necessarily resulted the
heightened temperature; this contact again depended
upon a preceding change, for instance the sun's rays falling
upon a burning-glass; this again upon the removal of a
cloud from before the sun; this upon the wind; the wind
upon the unequal density of the atmosphere; this upon

other conditions, and so forth *in infinitum*. When a state contains all the requisite conditions for bringing about a new state excepting *one, this one,* when at last it arrives, is, in a sense, rightly called the cause κατ᾽ ἐξοχήν, inasmuch as we here have the final—in this case the decisive—change especially in view; but if we leave out this consideration, no single condition of the causal state has any advantage over the rest with reference to the determination of the causal connection in general, merely because it happens to be the last. Thus the removal of the cloud in the above example, is in so far the cause of the igniting, as it took place later than the direction of the burning-glass towards the object; but this might have taken place after the removal of the cloud and the addition of oxygen might have occurred later still: in this respect therefore it is the accidental order of things that determines which is the cause. On closer inspection, however, we find that it is *the entire state* which is the cause of the ensuing one, so that the chronological order in which its single conditions were brought about, is in all essential respects indifferent. With reference to a given case therefore, the last occurring condition of a state may be called the cause κατ᾽ ἐξοχήν, because it completes the measure of the necessary conditions, and its appearance thus becomes the decisive change. For purposes of general consideration, however, it is only the *entire* state which, by bringing about its successor, can be regarded as the cause. The single requisites which, added together, complete and constitute the cause may be called causal elements (*ursächliche Momente*) or even *conditions*, and into these accordingly the cause may be subdivided. On the other hand, it is quite wrong to call the objects themselves causes, instead of the states: some would, for instance, call the burning-glass in the above example the cause of the ignition; while others, again, would call the cloud the cause; others the sun or the

oxygen, and so on arbitrarily and without order. But it is
absurd to call an object the cause of another object; first of
all, because objects not only contain form and quality, but
Matter also, which has neither beginning or end; secondly,
because the law of causality refers exclusively to *changes*,
i.e. to the entrance and exit of states in Time, wherein it
regulates that special relation, in reference to which the
earlier state is called *cause*, the later *effect*, and the necessary connection between both, the *resulting* of the one
from the other.

I here refer the thoughtful reader to the explanations I
have given in my chief work.[1] For it is of the highest importance that our conception of the true and proper meaning of the law of causality and the sphere of its validity
should be perfectly clear and definite: before all things,
that we should recognize, that this law refers solely and
exclusively to *changes* of material states and to nothing
else whatever; consequently, that it ought not to be
brought in when *these* are not in question. The law of
causality is the regulator of the *changes* undergone in
Time by objects of our outer *experience;* but these objects
are all material. Each change can only be brought about
by another having preceded it, which is determined by a
rule, and then the new change takes place as being necessarily induced by the preceding one. This necessity is the
causal nexus.

However simple therefore the law of causality is, we
nevertheless find it expressed quite differently in all philosophical manuals, from the earliest down to the latest
ages : namely, in a broader, more abstract, therefore less
definite way. We are, for instance, informed, now, that it
is that by which something else comes into being; now,
that it is what produces another thing or gives it reality,

[1] " Die Welt a. W. u. V." vol. ii. chap. 4, especially p. 42 and *seq.* of
the 2nd edition ; p. 46 *seq.* of the 3rd edition.

&c. &c. Wolf says: *Causa est principium, a quo exis-tentia, sive actualitas, entis alterius dependet;* whereas it is obvious that in causality we have only to do with changes in the form of uncreated, indestructible Matter, and that a springing into existence of what did not previously exist is an impossibility. Want of clearness of thought may, no doubt, in most cases have led to these views of the causal relation; but surely sometimes an *arrière-pensée* lurks in the background—a theological intention coqueting with the Cosmological Proof, for whose sake it is ready to falsify even transcendental, *à priori* truths, the mother's milk of human understanding. We find the clearest instance of this in Thomas Brown's book, "On the Rela-tion of Cause and Effect," a work of 460 pages, which, in 1835, had already reached its fourth edition, and has pro-bably since gone through several more, and which, in spite of its wearisome, pedantic, rambling prolixity, does not handle the subject badly. Now this Englishman rightly recognises, that it is invariably with *changes* that the causal law has to do, and that every effect is accordingly a *change.* Yet, although it can hardly have escaped him, he is unwilling to admit that every cause is likewise a *change,* and that the whole process is therefore nothing but the uninterrupted nexus of *changes* succeeding one another in Time. On the contrary, he persists in clumsily calling the cause an *object* or *substance,* which precedes the change, and in tormenting himself throughout his tedious book with this entirely false expression, which spoils all his explanations, notwithstanding his own better knowledge and against his conscience, simply in order that his defini-tion may on no account stand in the way of the Cosmo-logical Proof, which others might hereafter state elsewhere. —But what can a truth be worth which needs devices such as these to prepare its way?

And what have our own worthy, honest German pro-

fessors of philosophy been doing in behalf of their dearly
beloved Cosmological Proof, since Kant dealt it the death-
blow in his Critique of Pure Reason?—they, who prize
truth above everything. They were, indeed, at their wits'
ends, for—as these worthies well know, though they do not
say so—*causa prima* is, just as well as *causa sui*, a *contradictio in adjecto*, albeit the former expression is more
generally used than the latter. It is besides usually
pronounced with a very serious, not to say solemn,
air; nay, many people, especially English Reverends, turn
up their eyes in a truly edifying way when they im-
pressively and emphatically mention that *contradictio in
adjecto :* 'the first cause.' They know that a first cause
is just as inconceivable as the point at which Space
ends or the moment when Time first began. For every
cause is a *change*, which necessarily obliges us to ask for
the preceding change that brought it about, and so on *in
infinitum, in infinitum !* Even a first state of Matter, from
which, as it has ceased to be, all following states could
have proceeded, is inconceivable. For if this state had in
itself been the cause of the following ones, they must likewise have existed from all eternity, and the actual state
existing at the present moment could not have only just
now come into being. If, on the other hand, that first
state only began to be causal at some given period, something or other must have *changed* it, for its inactivity to
have ceased; but then something must have occurred,
some change must have taken place ; and this again
obliges us to ask for its cause—*i.e.* a change which preceded it; and here we are once more on the causal ladder,
up which we are whipped step by step, higher and higher,
in infinitum, in infinitum ! (These gentlemen will surely
not have the face to talk to me of Matter itself arising out
of nothing ! If so, they will find corollaries at their service
further on.) The causal law therefore is not so accom-

modating as to let itself be used like a hired cab, which we dismiss when we have reached our destination; rather does it resemble the broom brought to life by the apprentice-wizard in Göthe's poem,[1] which, when once set in motion, does not leave off running and fetching water until the old master-wizard himself stops it, which he alone has the power to do. These gentlemen, however, have no master-wizards among them. So what did they do, these noble, genuine lovers of truth, ever on the alert, of course, to proclaim the advent of real merit to the world as soon as it shows itself in their profession, who far from wishing to divert attention from the works of those who are really what *they* only seem to be, by craftily ignoring and meanly keeping them dark, are naturally foremost to acknowledge their worth—aye, surely, as surely as folly loves wisdom above everything? What did they do, I say, to help their old friend, the sorely distressed Cosmological Proof, now at its last gasp? Oh, they hit upon a shrewd device. "Friend," they said, "you are in sorry plight since your fatal encounter with that stubborn old man in Königsberg, and indeed your brethren, the Ontological and Physico-theological Proofs are in no better condition. Never mind, you shall not be abandoned by us (that is what we are paid for, you know); only you must alter your dress and your name—there is no help for it—for if we call you by your right name, every-one will take to his heels. Now *incognito*, on the contrary, we can take you by the arm, and once more lead you into society; only, as we have just said, it must be *incognito!* That is sure to answer! First of all, your argument must henceforth be called *The Absolute*. This has a foreign, dignified, aristocratic ring; and no one knows better than we do all that can be done with Germans by assuming airs of importance. Of course all know what the real meaning

[1] Göthe, " Der Zauberlehrling."

is, and pique themselves upon that knowledge. But you
yourself must come forward disguised, in the form of an
enthymeme. Be sure and leave behind you all those pro-
syllogisms and premisses, by which you used to drag us
wearily up the long climax, for everyone knows how utterly
useless they are. Come forward with a bold face and a
self-sufficient, supercilious air, like a man of few words,
and at one bound you will reach the goal. Exclaim (and
we will chime in), '*The Absolute*, confound it! *that* must
exist, or there would be nothing at all!' Here, strike
the table with your fist. Whence does the Absolute
come? 'What a silly question! Did not I tell you
it was the Absolute?'—That will do, forsooth! That
will do! Germans are accustomed to content themselves
with words instead of thoughts. Do we not train them
to it from their cradle? Only look at Hegelianism!
What is it but empty, hollow, nauseous twaddle! Yet
how brilliant a career was that of this philosophical
time-server! A few mercenary individuals had only to
strike up a laudation of this stuff, and they at once
found an echo to their voices in the empty hollow of a
thousand numskulls—an echo which still continues to re-
sound, and to extend—and behold! an ordinary intellect,
a common impostor soon became a sublime thinker. Take
heart, therefore! Besides, our friend and patron, we will
also second you in other ways, for how, indeed, are we to
get a living without you? So that carping old faultfinder,
Kant, has been criticizing Reason, and clipping her wings,
has he? Well, then, we will invent a *new* sort of Reason,
such as has never been heard of—a Reason that does not
think, but which has direct intuition—a Reason which sees
Ideas (a high-flown word, made to mystify), sees them
bodily; or which apprehends directly that which you and
others seek to prove; or, again, a Reason which has
forebodings of all this—this last for the benefit of those

who do not care to make large concessions, but also are
satisfied with very little.   Let us thus pass off early incul-
cated, popular conceptions for direct revelations of this
new kind of Reason, *i.e.* for inspirations from above.   As
for that old-fashioned Reason, which criticism has criticized away, let us degrade it, call it Understanding, and
send it about its business.   Well, and what is to become
of real, true Understanding?—What in the world have
we to do with real, true Understanding?—You smile in-
credulously; but we know our listeners, and the *harum,*
horum we see on the students' benches before us.   Bacon
of Verulam already in his time said : 'Young men learn to
believe at Universities.'   Of this they can learn as much as
they wish from us; we have a good stock of articles of
faith on hand.   Should any misgivings assail you, remember that we are in Germany, where what would have
been impossible in any other country, has been found
possible: where a dull-witted, ignorant, pseudo-philosopher,
whose ineffably hollow verbiage disorganizes peoples'
brains completely and permanently, a scribbler of nonsense—I am speaking of our dearly beloved Hegel—has
not only been actually proclaimed a profound thinker with
impunity, and even without incurring ridicule, but is
readily accepted as such : yes, indeed, for this fiction has
found credence for the last thirty years, and is believed to
this day!—Once therefore we have this Absolute with
your help, we are quite safe, in spite of Kant and his
Critique.—We may then philosophise in a lofty tone,
making the Universe proceed from *the Absolute* by means
of the most heterogeneous deductions, one more tiresome
than the other—this, by the way, being their only point of
resemblance.   We can call the world the Finite, and the
Absolute the Infinite—thus giving an agreeable variety to
our nonsense—and talk of nothing but God, explaining
how, why, wherefore, by what voluntary or involuntary

process he created or brought forth the world, showing whether he be within or without it, and so forth, as if Philosophy were Theology, and as if it sought for enlightenment concerning God, not concerning the Universe!"

The Cosmological Proof, with which we here have to do, and to which the above 'apostrophe is addressed, consists thus, properly speaking, in the assertion, that the principle of the sufficient reason of *becoming*, or the law of causality, necessarily leads to a thought which destroys it and declares it to be null and void. For the *causa prima* (*absolutum*) can only be reached by proceeding upwards from consequence to reason, through a series prolonged *ad libitum ;* but it is impossible to stop short at the *causa prima* without at once annulling the principle of sufficient reason.

Having thus briefly and clearly shown the nullity of the Cosmological Proof, as I had in my second chapter already shown the nullity of the Ontological Proof, the sympathizing reader may perhaps expect me to do the same with respect to the Physico-theological Proof, which is a great deal more plausible. As, however, this belongs by its nature to a different department of philosophy, it would be quite out of place here. I therefore refer him to Kant's Critique of Pure Reason, as well as to his Critique of the Faculty of Judgment, where he treats this subject *ex professo ;* I likewise refer him, as a complement to Kant's purely negative procedure, to my own positive one in "The Will in Nature," [1] a work which, though small in bulk, is rich and weighty in content. As for the indifferent reader, he is free to let this and indeed all my writings pass down unread to his descendants. It matters not to me ; for I am here, not for one generation only, but for many.

Now, as the law of causality is known to us *à priori*, and is therefore a transcendental law, applicable to every possible

[1] The translation of which follows the Fourfold Root in the present volume.

experience and consequently without exception, as will be
shown in § 21; as moreover it decides, that upon a given,
definite, relatively first state, a second equally definite one
inevitably ensues by rule, *i.e.*, always; the relation between
cause and effect is a necessary one, so that the causal law
authorizes us to form hypothetical judgments, and thereby
shows itself to be a form of the principle of sufficient
reason, upon which principle all judgments must be founded
and, as will be shown further on, all *necessity* is based.

This form of our principle I call the *principle of the
sufficient reason of becoming*, because its application invariably pre-supposes a change, the entering upon a new
state: consequently a becoming. One of its essential characteristics is this: that the cause always precedes the effect in
Time (compare § 47), and this alone gives us the original
criterion by which to distinguish which is cause and which
effect, of two states linked together by the causal nexus.
Conversely, in some cases, the causal nexus is known to us
through former experience; but the rapidity with which
the different states follow upon each other is so great, that
the order in which this happens escapes our perception.
We then conclude with complete certitude from causality
to succession: thus, for instance, we infer that the igniting
of gunpowder precedes its explosion.[1]

From this essential connection between causality and
succession it follows, that the conception of reciprocity,
strictly speaking, has no meaning; for it presumes the
effect to be again the cause of its cause: that is, that
what follows is at the same time what precedes. In a
"Critique of Kantian Philosophy," which I have added to
my chief work, and to which I refer my readers,[2] I have

---

[1] Here I refer my readers to "Die Welt als Wille und Vorstellung,"
vol. ii. chap. 4, p. 41 of the 2nd edition, and p. 45 of the 3rd edition.

[2] "Die Welt a. W. u. V." vol. i. pp. 517-521 of the 2nd edition, and
pp. 544-549 of the 3rd edition.

shown at length that this favourite conception is inadmissible. It may be remarked, that authors usually have recourse to it just when their insight is becoming less clear, and this accounts for the frequency of its use. Nay, it is precisely when a writer comes to the end of his conceptions, that the word '*reciprocity*' presents itself more readily than any other; it may, in fact, be looked upon as a kind of alarm-gun, denoting that the author has got out of his depth. It is also worthy of remark, that the word *Wechselwirkung*, literally reciprocal action—or, as we have preferred translating it, *reciprocity*—is only found in the German language, and that there is no precise equivalent for it in daily use in any other tongue.

From the law of causality spring two corollaries which, in virtue of this origin, are accredited as cognitions *à priori*, therefore as unquestionable and without exception. They are, *the law of inertia* and that *of permanence of substance*. The first of these laws avers, that every state in which a body can possibly be—consequently that of repose as well as that of any kind of movement—must last for ever without change, diminution, or augmentation, unless some cause supervenes to alter or annul it. But the other law, by which the eternity of Matter is affirmed, results from the fact, that the law of causality is exclusively applicable to *states* of bodies, such as repose, movement, form, and quality, since it presides over their temporal passing in or out of being; but that it is by no means applicable to the existence of *that which endures* these states, and is called *Substance*, in order precisely to express its exemption from all arising and perishing. '*Substance is permanent*' means, that it can neither pass into, nor out of being: so that its quantity existing in the universe can neither be increased nor diminished. That we know this *à priori*, is proved by the consciousness of unassailable certainty with which, when we see a body disappear—whether it be by conjuring, by minute subdivision,

by combustion, volatilisation, or indeed any process whatever—we all nevertheless firmly assume that its substance, *i.e.* its *matter*, must still exist somewhere or other
in undiminished quantity, whatever may have become
of its *form ;* likewise, when we perceive a body suddenly in
a place where it was not before, that it must have been
brought there or formed by some combination of invisible
particles—for instance, by precipitation—but that it, *i.e.*
its substance, cannot have then started into existence;
for this implies a total impossibility and is utterly inconceivable. The certainty with which we assume this beforehand (*à priori*), proceeds from the fact, that our Understanding possesses absolutely no form under which to conceive
the beginning and end of Matter.   For, as before said, the
law of causality—the only form in which we are able to
conceive changes at all—is solely applicable to *states* of
bodies, and never under any circumstances to the existence
of *that which undergoes* all changes : *Matter.* This is why I
place the principle of the permanence of Matter among the
corollaries of the causal law.   Moreover, we cannot have
acquired *à posteriori* the conviction that substance is permanent, partly because it cannot, in most instances, be
empirically established ; partly also, because every empirical knowledge obtained exclusively by means of induction, has only approximate, consequently precarious, never
unconditioned, certainty. The firmness of our persuasion as
to this principle is therefore of a different kind and nature
from our security of conviction with regard to the accuracy
of any *empirically* discovered law of Nature, since it has an
entirely different, perfectly unshakable, never vacillating
firmness.   The reason of this is, that the principle expresses a *transcendental* knowledge, *i.e.* one which determines and fixes, *prior* to all experience, what is in any way
possible within the whole range of experience ; but, precisely by this, it reduces the world of experience to a mere

cerebral phenomenon. Even the most universal among
the non-transcendental laws of Nature and the one least
liable to exception—the law of gravitation—is of empirical
origin, consequently without guarantee as to its absolute
universality; wherefore it is still from time to time called
in question, and doubts occasionally arise as to its validity
beyond our solar system; and astronomers carefully call
attention to any indications corroborative of its doubtful-
ness with which they may happen to meet, thereby showing that they regard it as merely empirical. The question
may of course be raised, whether gravitation takes effect
between bodies which are separated by an *absolute* vacuum,
or whether its action within a solar system may not be
mediated by some sort of ether, and may not cease altogether between fixed stars; but these questions only admit
of an empirical solution, and this proves that here we have
not to do with a knowledge *à priori*. If, on the other hand,
we admit with Kant and Laplace the hypothesis, as the
most probable one, that each solar system has developed
out of an original *nebula* by a gradual process of condensa-
tion, we still cannot for a moment conceive the possibility
of that original substance having sprung into being
out of *nothing :* we are forced to assume the anterior
existence of its particles somewhere or other, as well as
their having been brought together somehow or other,
precisely because of the transcendental nature of the principle of the permanence of Substance. In my Critique
of Kantian Philosophy,[1] I have shown at length, that
Substance is but another word for *Matter*, the conception of
substance not being realisable excepting in *Matter*, and
therefore deriving its origin from *Matter*, and I have also
specially pointed out how that conception was formed
solely to serve a surreptitious purpose. Like many other

[1] " Die Welt a. W. u. V." vol. i. p. 550 of 2nd, and 580 of 3rd
edition.

equally certain truths, this eternity of Matter (called the permanence of substance) is forbidden fruit for professors of philosophy ; so they slip past it with a bashful, sidelong glance.

By the endless chain of causes and effects which directs all *changes* but never extends beyond them, two existing things remain untouched, precisely because of the limited range of its action : on the one hand, *Matter*, as we have just shown; on the other hand, the primary *forces of Nature*. The first (matter) remains uninfluenced by the causal nexus, because it is *that which undergoes* all changes, or *on which* they take place ; the second (the primary forces), because it is they alone *by which* changes or effects become possible; for they alone give causality to causes, *i.e.* the faculty of operating, which the causes therefore hold as mere vassals a fief.   Cause and effect are *changes* connected together to necessary succession in Time ; whereas the forces of Nature by means of which all causes operate, are exempt from all change ; in this sense therefore they are outside Time, but precisely on that account they are always and everywhere in reserve, omnipresent and inexhaustible, ever ready to manifest themselves, as soon as an opportunity presents itself in the thread of causality.   A *cause*, like its *effect*, is invariably something individual, a single change ; whereas a force of Nature is something universal, unchangeable, present at all times and in all places.   The attraction of a thread by amber, for instance, at the present moment, is an effect ; its cause is the preceding friction and actual contact of the amber with the thread ; and the *force of Nature* which acts in, and presides over, the process, is Electricity.   The explanation of this matter is to be found in my chief work,[1] and there I have shown in a long chain of causes and effects

[1] See "Die Welt a. W. u. V." vol. i. § 26, p. 153 of the 2nd, and p. 160 of the 3rd edition.

how the most heterogeneous natural forces successively come into play in them. By this explanation the difference between transitory phenomena and permanent forms of operation, becomes exceedingly clear; and as, moreover, a whole section (§ 26) is devoted to the question, it will be sufficient here to give a brief sketch of it. The *rule*, by which a force of Nature manifests itself in the chain of causes and effects—consequently the link which connects it with them—is the law of Nature. But the confusion between forces of Nature and causes is as frequent as it is detrimental to clearness of thought. It seems indeed as though no one had accurately defined the difference between these conceptions before me, however great may have been the urgency for such a distinction. Not only are forces of Nature turned into causes by such expressions as, 'Electricity, Gravity, &c., are the *cause* of so-and-so,' but they are even often turned into effects by those who search for a cause for Electricity, Gravity, &c. &c., which is absurd. Diminishing the number of the forces of Nature, however, by reducing one to another, as for instance Magnetism is in our days reduced to Electricity, is a totally different thing. Every *true*, consequently really primary force of Nature—and every fundamental chemical property belongs to these forces—is essentially a *qualitas occulta*, *i.e.* it does not admit of physical, but only of metaphysical explanation : in other words, of an explanation which transcends the world of phenomena. No one has carried this confusion, or rather identification, of causes with forces of Nature further than Maine de Biran in his "Nouvelles considérations des rapports du physique au moral," for it is essential to his philosophy. It is besides remarkable, that when he speaks of causes, he rarely uses the word *cause* alone, but almost always speaks of *cause ou force*, just as we have seen Spinoza above (§ 8) write *ratio sive causa* no less than eight times in the same page. Both writers are evidently conscious that they are identifying two disparates, in order to be able to make use of the one or the other, according to circumstances ; for this end they are obliged to keep the identification constantly before their readers' mind.—

Now Causality, as the director of each and every change, presents itself in Nature under *three* distinct forms : as *causes* in the strictest acceptation of the word, as *stimuli*, and as *motives*. It is just upon this difference that the real, essential distinction between inorganic bodies, plants, and animals is based, and not upon external, anatomical, let alone chemical, distinctions.

A *cause*, in its narrowest sense, is that upon which changes in the *inorganic* kingdom alone ensue : those changes, that is to say, which form the theme of Mechanics, Physics, and Chemistry. Newton's third fundamental law, "Action and reaction are equal to one another," applies exclusively to this cause, and enunciates, that the state which precedes (the cause) undergoes a change equivalent to that produced by it (the effect). In this form of causality alone, moreover, does the degree of the effect always exactly correspond to the degree of the cause, so as to enable us accurately to calculate the one by means of the other.

The second form of causality is the *stimulus ;* it reigns over *organic* life, as such, *i.e.* over plant life and the vegetative, that is, the unconscious, part of animal life. This second form is characterized by the absence of the distinctive signs of the first. In it accordingly action and reaction are not equal, nor does the intensity of the effect by any means correspond throughout all its degrees to the intensity of the cause ; in fact, the opposite effect may even be produced by intensifying the cause.

The third form of causality is the *motive*. Under this form causality rules animal life proper : that is, the exte-

rior, consciously performed actions of all animals. The
medium for motives is *knowledge* : an intellect is accordingly needed for susceptibility to motives. The true
characteristic of the animal is therefore the faculty of
knowing, of representing (*Das Vorstellen*). Animals, as
such, always move towards some aim and end, which
therefore must have been *recognised* by them : that is to
say, it must have presented itself to them as something different from themselves, yet of which they are
conscious. Therefore the proper definition of the animal
would be : 'That which knows;' for no other definition
quite hits the mark or can even perhaps stand the test of
investigation. Movement induced by motives is necessarily
wanting where there is no cognitive faculty, and movement
by stimuli alone remains, *i.e.* plant life. Irritability and
sensibility are therefore inseparable. Still motives evidently act in a different way from stimuli ; for the action
of the former may be very brief, nay, need only be
momentary ; since their efficacy, unlike that of stimuli,
stands in no relation whatever to the duration of that
action, to the proximity of the object, &c. &c. A motive
needs but to be perceived therefore, to take effect ; whereas
stimuli always require outward, often even inward, contact
and invariably a certain length of time.

This short sketch of the three forms of causality will
suffice here. They are more fully described in my Prize-
essay on Free Will.[1] One thing, however, still remains to
be urged. The difference between cause, stimulus, and
motive, is obviously only a consequence of the various
degrees of *receptivity* of beings ; the greater their receptivity, the feebler may be the nature of the influence : a stone
needs an impact, while man obeys a look. Nevertheless,
both are moved by a sufficient cause, therefore with the

---

[1] See " Die beiden Grundprobleme der Ethik," p. 30-34.

same necessity.   For ' *motivation* ' [1] is only causality pass-ing through knowledge ; the intellect is the medium of the motives, because it is the highest degree of receptivity.   By this, however, the law of causality loses nothing whatever of its rigour and certainty ; for motives are causes and operate with the same necessity which all causes bring with them.   This necessity is easy to perceive in animals because of the greater simplicity of their intellect, which is limited to the perception of what is present.   Man's in-tellect is double : for not only has he intuitive, but abstract, knowledge, which last is not limited to what is present. Man possesses Reason ; he therefore has a power of elective decision with clear consciousness : that is, he is able to weigh against one another motives which exclude each other, as such ; in other terms, he can let them try their strength on his will.   The most powerful motive then decides him, and his actions ensue with just the same necessity as the roll-ing of a ball after it has been struck.   Freedom of Will [2] means (not professorial twaddle but) " *that a given human being, in a given situation, can act in two different ways.*" But the utter absurdity of this assertion is a truth as certain and as clearly proved, as any truth can be which passes the limits of pure mathematics.   In my Essay on Free Will, to which the Norwegian Society awarded the prize, this truth is demonstrated more clearly, methodi-cally, and thoroughly than has been done before by anyone else, and this moreover with special reference to those facts of our consciousness by which ignorant people imagine that absurdity to be confirmed.   In all that is essential however, Hobbes, Spinoza, Priestley, Voltaire,

----

[1] The word "motivation," though it may appear objectionable to the English reader, seemed unavoidable here, as being Schopenhauer's own term, for which there is no adequate equivalent in general use in our language. [Translator's note.]

[2] Here used in the absolute sense of *liberum arbitrium in differentiæ.* [Tr.]

and even Kant [1] already taught the same doctrine. Our professional philosophers, of course, do not let this interfere with their holding forth on Free Will, as if it were an understood thing which had never been questioned. But what do these gentlemen imagine the above-named great men to have come into the world for, by the grace of Nature? To enable them (the professors) to earn their livelihood by philosophy?—Since I had proved this truth in my prize-essay more clearly than had ever been done before, and since moreover a Royal Society had sanctioned that proof by placing my essay among its memoranda, it surely behoved these worthies, considering the views they held, to make a vigorous attack upon so pernicious a doctrine, so detestable a heresy, and thoroughly to refute it. Nay, this duty was all the more imperative

---

[1] " Whatever conception one may form of freedom of the will, for metaphysical purposes, its phenomena, human actions, are nevertheless determined by universal laws of Nature, just as well as every other occurrence in Nature." " Ideen zu einer allgemeinen Geschichte." Anfang. I. Kant. " All the acts of a man, so far as they are phenomena, are determined from his empirical character and from the other concomitant causes, according to the order of Nature; and if we could investigate all the manifestations of his will to the very bottom, there would be not a single human action which we could not predict with certainty and recognize from its preceding conditions as necessary. There is no freedom therefore with reference to this empirical character, and yet it is only with reference to it that we can consider man, when we are merely *observing*, and, as is the case in anthropology, trying to investigate the motive causes of his actions physiologically."—" Kritik. d. r. Vern." p. 549 of the 1st edition, and p. 577 of the 5th edition. (Engl. Transl. by M. Müller, p. 474.)

" It may therefore be taken for granted, that if we could see far enough into a man's mode of thinking, as it manifests itself in his inner, as well as outer actions, for us to know every, even the faintest motive, and in like manner all the other causes which act upon these, it would be possible to calculate his conduct in future with the same certainty as an eclipse of the sun or moon."—" Kritik. der praktischen Vernunft " ed. Rosenkranz, p. 230 and p. 177 of the 4th edition.

as, in my other essay " On the Foundation of Morality," [1]
I had proved the utter groundlessness of Kant's practical
Reason with its Categorical Imperative which, under the
name of the Moral Law, is still used by these gentlemen as
the corner-stone of their own shallow systems of morality.
I have shown it to be a futile assumption so clearly and
irrefutably, that no one with a spark of judgment can
possibly believe any longer in this fiction.—" Well, and so
they probably did."—Oh no! They take good care not to
venture on such slippery ground! Their ability consists in
holding their tongues; silence is all they have to oppose
to intelligence, earnestness, and truth. In not one of the
products of their useless scribblings that have appeared
since 1841, has the slightest notice been taken of my
Ethics—undoubtedly the most important work on Moral
Philosophy that has been published for the last sixty
years—nay, their terror of me and of my truth is so great,
that none of the literary journals issued by Academies or
Universities has so much as mentioned the book. *Zitto,
zitto*, lest the public should perceive anything: in this
consists the whole of their policy. The instinct of self-
preservation may, no doubt, be at the bottom of these
artful tactics. For would not a philosophy, whose sole aim
was truth, and which had no other consideration in view,
be likely to play the part of the iron pot among the
earthen ones, were it to come in contact with the petty
systems composed under the influence of a thousand personal considerations by people whose chief qualification is
the propriety of their sentiments? Their wretched fear of
my writings is the fear of truth. Nor can it be denied,
that precisely this very doctrine of the complete necessity
of all acts of the will stands in flagrant contradiction with
all the hypotheses of their favourite old-woman's philo-

---

[1] Published in the same volume with the Prize-Essay on " Free
Will." See " Die beiden Grundprobleme der Ethik."

sophy cut after the pattern of Judaism. Still, that severely
tested truth, far from being disturbed by all this, as a
sure datum and criterion, as a true δός μοι ποῦ στῶ, proves
the futility of all that old-woman's philosophy and the
urgent need of a fundamentally different, incomparably
deeper view of the Universe and of Man;—no matter
whether that view be compatible with the official duties
of a professional philosopher or not.

§ 21. À priori *character of the conception of Causality.* *Intellectual Character of Empirical Perception.*

THE UNDERSTANDING.

In the professorial philosophy of our philosophy-pro-
fessors we are still taught to this day, that perception of the
outer world is a thing of the senses, and then there follows a long dissertation upon each of the five senses;
whereas no mention whatever is made of the intellectual
character of perception: that is to say, of the fact, that it
is mainly the work of the Understanding, which, by means
of its own peculiar form of Causality, together with the
forms of pure sensibility, Time and Space, which are pos-
tulated by Causality, primarily creates and produces the
objective, outer world out of the raw material of a few sensations. And yet in its principal features, I had stated
this matter in the first edition of the present treatise [1]
and soon after developed it more fully in my treatise " On
Vision and Colours" (1816), of which Professor Rosas has
shown his appreciation by allowing it to lead him into
plagiarism. [2] But our professors of philosophy have not

[1] Anno 1813, pp. 53-55.
[2] For further details see my " Will in Nature," p. 19 of the 1st edition,
and p. 14 of the 3rd. (P. 230 *et seqq.* of the translation of the " Will in
Nature," which follows the " Fourfold Root " in the present volume.)

thought fit to take the slightest notice either of this, or indeed of any of the other great and important truths which
it has been the aim and labour of my whole life to set
forth, in order to secure them as a lasting possession to
mankind. It does not suit their tastes, or fit into their
notions; it leads to no Theology, nor is it even adapted to
drill students for higher State purposes. In short, professional philosophers do not care to learn from me, nor do they
even see how much they might learn from me : that is, all
that their children and their children's children will learn
from me. They prefer to sit down and spin a long metaphysical yarn, each out of his own thoughts, for the benefit
of the public; and no doubt, if fingers are a sufficient
qualification, they have it. How right was Macchiavelli
when he said, as Hesiod [1] before him : "There are three
sorts of heads : firstly, those which acquire knowledge of
things and comprehend them by themselves; secondly,
those which recognise the truth when it is shown them by
others; and thirdly, those which can do neither the one
nor the other." [2]—

One must indeed be forsaken by all the gods, to imagine
that the outer, perceptible world, filling Space in its three
dimensions and moving on in the inexorable flow of Time,
governed at every step by the laws of Causality, which is
without exception, and in all this merely obeying laws we
can indicate before all experience of them—that such a
world as this, we say, can have a real, objective existence
outside us, without any agency of our own, and that it can
then have found its way into our heads through bare sensation and thus have a second existence within us like the
one outside. For what a miserably poor thing is mere
sensation, after all ! Even in the noblest of our organs it
is nothing but a local, specific feeling, susceptible of some

[1] Hesiod, ἔργα, 293.
[2] Macchiavelli, "Il principe," cap. 22.

slight variation, still in itself always subjective and, as such therefore, incapable of containing anything objective, anything like perception. For sensation is and remains a process within the organism and is limited, as such, to the region within the skin; it cannot therefore contain anything which lies beyond that region, or, in other words, anything that is outside us. A sensation may be pleasant or unpleasant—which betokens a relation to the Will— but nothing objective can ever lie in any sensation. In the organs of the senses, sensation is heightened by the confluence of the nerve-extremities, and can easily be excited from without on account of their extensive distribution and the delicacy of the envelope which encloses them; it is besides specially susceptible to particular influences, such as light, sound, smell; notwithstanding which it is and remains mere sensation, like all others within our body, consequently something essentially subjective, of whose changes we only become immediately conscious in the form of the *inner* sense, Time : that is, successively. It is only when the *Understanding* begins to act—a function, not of single, delicate nerve-extremities, but of that mysterious, complicated structure weighing from five to ten pounds, called the brain—only when it begins to apply its sole form, *the causal law*, that a powerful transformation takes place, by which subjective sensation becomes objective perception. For, in virtue of its own peculiar form, therefore *à priori*, *i.e. before* all experience (since there could have been none till then), the Understanding conceives the given corporeal sensation as an *effect* (a word which the Understanding alone comprehends), which effect, as such, necessarily implies a *cause*. Simultaneously it summons to its assistance *Space*, the form of the *outer* sense, lying likewise ready in the intellect (*i.e.* the brain), in order to remove that cause *beyond* the organism ; for it is by this that the external world first arises, Space alone rendering it pos-

sïble, so that pure intuition à *priori* has to supply the
foundation for empirical perception.   In this process, as
I shall soon show more clearly, the Understanding avails
itself of all the several data, even the minutest, which are
presented to it by the given sensation, in order to construct
the cause of it in Space in conformity with them. This intellectual operation (which is moreover explicitly denied both
by Schelling [1] and by Fries [2]), does not however take place
discursively or reflectively, *in abstracto*, by means of conceptions and words; it is, on the contrary, an intuitive and
quite direct process.   For by it alone, therefore exclusively
in the Understanding and *for* the Understanding, does
the real, objective, corporeal world, filling Space in its
three dimensions, present itself and further proceed, according to the same law of causality, to change in Time,
and to move in Space.—It is therefore the Understanding
itself which has to create the objective world; for this
world cannot walk into our brain from outside all ready
cut and dried through the senses and the openings of their
organs.   In fact, the senses supply nothing but the raw
materials which the Understanding at once proceeds to
work up into the objective view of a corporeal world, subject to regular laws, by means of the simple forms we have
indicated : Space, Time, and Causality.   Accordingly our
every-day *empirical perception* is an *intellectual* one and has
a right to claim this predicate, which German pseudo-philosophers have given to a pretended intuition of dream-worlds,
in which their beloved *Absolute* is supposed to perform its
evolutions.   And now I will proceed to show how wide is
the gulf which separates sensation from perception, by
pointing out how raw is the material out of which the
beautiful edifice is constructed.

---

[1] Schelling, " Philosophische Schriften " (1809), vol. i. pp. 237 and 238.
[2] Fries, " Kritik der Vernunft," vol. i. pp. 52-56 and p. 290 of the 1st
edition.

Objective perception makes use, properly speaking, of only two senses; touch and sight. These alone supply the data upon which, as its basis, the Understanding constructs the objective world by the process just described. The three other senses remain on the whole subjective; for their sensations, while pointing to an external cause, still contain no data by which its relations *in Space* can be determined. Now *Space* is the form of all perception, *i.e.* of *that* apprehension, in which alone *objects* can, properly speaking, present themselves. Therefore those other three senses can no doubt serve to announce the presence of objects we already know in some other way; but no construction in Space, consequently no objective perception, can possibly be founded on their data. A rose cannot be constructed from its perfume, and a blind man may hear music all his life without having the slightest objective representation either of the musicians, or of the instruments, or of the vibrations of the air. On the other hand, the sense of hearing is of great value as a medium for language, and through this it is the sense of *Reason*. It is also valuable as a medium for music, which is the only way in which we comprehend numerical relations not only *in abstracto*, but directly, *in concreto*. A musical sound or tone, however, gives no clue to spacial relations, therefore it never helps to bring the nature of its cause nearer to us; we stop short at it, so that it is no datum for the Understanding in its construction of the objective world. The sensations of touch and sight alone are such data; therefore a blind man without either hands or feet, while able to construct Space for himself *à priori* in all its regularity, would nevertheless acquire but a very vague representation of the objective world. Yet what is supplied by touch and sight is not by any means perception, but merely the raw material for it. For perception is so far from being contained in the sensations of touch and sight, that these sensations have not even the faintest resemblance to the qualities of the things which present themselves to us through them, as I shall presently show. Only what really belongs to sensation must first be clearly distinguished from what is added to it by the intellect in perception. In the beginning this is not easy, because we are so accustomed to pass from the sensation at once to its cause, that the cause presents itself to us without our noticing the sensation apart from it, by which, as it were, the premisses are supplied to this conclusion drawn by the Understanding.

Thus touch and sight have each their own special advantages, to begin with; therefore they assist each other mutually. Sight needs no contact, nor even proximity; its field is unbounded and extends to the stars. It is moreover sensitive to the most delicate degrees of light, shade, colour, and transparency; so that it supplies the Understanding with a quantity of nicely defined data, out of which, by dint of practice, it becomes able to construct the shape, size, distance, and nature of bodies, and represents them at once perceptibly. On the other hand, touch certainly depends upon contact; still its data are so varied and so trustworthy, that it is the most searching of all the senses. Even perception by sight may, in the last resort, be referred to touch; nay, sight may be looked upon as an imperfect touch extending to a great distance, which uses the rays of light as long feelers; and it is just because it is limited to those qualities which have light for their medium and is therefore one-sided, that it is so liable to deception; whereas touch supplies the data for cognising size, shape, hardness, softness, roughness, temperature, &c. &c., quite immediately. In this it is assisted, partly by the shape and mobility of our arms, hands, and fingers, from whose position in feeling objects the Understanding derives its data for constructing bodies in Space, partly by muscular power, which enables it to know the weight, solidity, toughness, or brittleness of bodies: all this with the least possible liability to error.

These data nevertheless do not by any means yet give perception, which is always the work of the Understanding, The sensation I have in pressing against a table with my hand, contains no representation of a firm cohesion of parts in that object, nor indeed anything at all like it. It is only when my Understanding passes from that sensation to its cause, that the intellect constructs for itself a body having the properties of solidity, impenetrability, and hardness. If in the dark, I put my hand upon a flat surface, or lay hold of a ball of about three inches in diameter, the same parts of my hand feel the pressure in both cases; it is only by the different position which my hand takes that, in the one or in the other case, my Understanding constructs the shape of the body whose contact is the cause of the sensation, for which it receives confirmation from the changes of position which I make. The sensations in the hand of a man born blind, on feeling an object of cubic shape, are quite uniform and the same on all sides and in every direction : the edges, it is true, press upon a smaller portion of his hand, still nothing at all like a cube is contained in these sensations. His Understanding, however, draws the immediate and intuitive conclusion from the resistance felt, that this resistance must have a cause, which then presents itself through that conclusion as a hard body; and through the movements of his arms in feeling the object, while the hand's sensation remains unaltered, he constructs the cubic shape in Space, which is known to him *à priori.* If the representation of a cause and of Space, together with their laws, had not already existed within him, the image of a cube could never have proceeded from those successive sensations in his hand. If a rope be drawn through his hand, he will construct, as the cause of the friction he feels and of its duration, a long cylindrical body, moving uniformly in the same direction in that particular position of his hand. But the representation of movement, *i.e.* of change of place in Space by means of Time, never could arise for him out of the mere sensation in his hand; for that sensation can neither contain, nor can it ever by itself alone produce any such thing. It is his intellect which must, on the contrary, contain within itself, before all experience, the intuitions of Space, Time, and together with them that of the possibility of movement; and it must also contain the representation of Causality, in order to pass from sensation—which alone is given by experience— to a cause of that sensation, and to construct that cause as a body having this or that shape, moving in this or that direction. For how great is the difference between a mere sensation in my hand and the representations of causality, materiality, and mobility in Space by means of Time! The sensation in my hand, even if its position and its points of contact are altered, is a thing far too uniform and far too poor in data, to enable me to construct out of it the representation of Space, with its three dimensions, and of the influences of bodies one upon another, together with the properties of expansion, impenetrability, cohesion, shape, hardness, softness, rest, and motion: the basis, in short, of the objective world. This is, on the contrary, only possible by the intellect containing within itself, anterior to all experience, Space, as the form of perception; Time, as the form of change; and the law of Causality, as the regulator of the passing in and out of changes. Now it is precisely the pre-existence before all experience of all these forms, which constitutes the Intellect. Physiologically, it is a function of the brain, which the brain no more learns by experience than the stomach to digest, or the liver to secrete bile. Besides, no other explanation can be given of the fact, that many who were born

blind, acquire a sufficiently complete knowledge of the relations of Space, to enable them to replace their want of eyesight by it to a considerable degree, and to perform astonish-
ing feats.   A hundred years ago Saunderson, for instance,
who was blind from his birth, lectured on Optics, Mathematics, and Astronomy at Cambridge.[1]   This, too, is the
only way to explain the exactly opposite case of Eva Lauk,
who was born without arms or legs, yet acquired an accurate
perception of the outer world by means of sight alone as
rapidly as other children.[2]   All this therefore proves that
Time, Space, and Causality are not conveyed into us by
touch or by sight, or indeed at all from outside, but that
they have an internal, consequently not empirical, but
intellectual origin.   From this again follows, that the perception of the bodily world is an essentially intellectual
process, a work of the Understanding, to which sensation
merely gives the opportunity and the data for application
in individual cases.

I shall now prove the same with regard to the sense of
sight.   Here the only immediate datum is the sensation
experienced by the retina, which, though admitting of great
variety, may still be reduced to the impression of light and
dark with their intermediate gradations and to that of
colours proper.   This sensation is entirely subjective: that
is to say, it only exists within the organism and under the
skin.   Without the Understanding, indeed, we should never
even become conscious of these gradations, excepting as of
peculiar, varied modifications of the feeling in our eye,
which would bear no resemblance to the shape, situation,
proximity, or distance of objects outside us.   For *sensation*,
in seeing, supplies nothing more than a varied affection of
the retina, exactly like the spectacle of a painter's palette

---

[1] Diderot, in his " Lettre sur les Aveugles," gives a detailed account
of Saunderson.
[2] See " Die Welt a. W. u. V." vol. ii. chap. 4.

with divers splashes of colour. Nor would anything more remain over in our consciousness, were we suddenly deprived of all our Understanding—let us say by paralysis of the brain—at a moment when we were contemplating a rich and extensive landscape, while the sensation was left unchanged : for this was the raw material out of which our Understanding had just before been constructing that perception.

Now, that the Understanding should thus be able, from such limited material as light, shade and colour, to produce the visible world, inexhaustibly rich in all its different shapes, by means of the simple function of referring effects to causes assisted by the intuition of Space, depends before all things upon the assistance given by the sensation itself, which consists in this : first, that the retina, as a surface, admits of a juxtaposition of impressions ; secondly, that light always acts in straight lines, and that its refraction in the eye itself is rectilinear ; finally, that the retina possesses the faculty of immediately feeling from which direction the light comes that impinges upon it, and this can, perhaps, only be accounted for by the rays of light penetrating below the surface of the retina. But by this we gain, that the mere impression at once indicates the direction of its cause ; that is, it points directly to the position of the object from which the light proceeds or is reflected. The passage to this object as a cause no doubt presupposes the knowledge of causal relations, as well as of the laws of Space ; but this knowledge constitutes precisely the furniture of the *Intellect*, which, here also, has again to create perception out of mere sensation. Let us now examine its procedure in doing so more closely.

The first thing it does is to set right the impression of the object, which is produced on the retina upside down. That original inversion is, as we know, brought about in the following manner. As each point of the visible object

sends forth its rays towards all sides in a rectilinear direction, the rays from its upper extremity cross those from its
lower extremity in the narrow aperture of the pupil, by
which the former impinge upon the bottom, the latter
upon the top, those projected from the right side upon the
left, and *vice versa.* The refracting apparatus of the eye,
which consists of the *humor aqueus, lens, et corpus vitreum,*
only serves to concentrate the rays of light proceeding from
the object, so as to find room for them on the small space
of the retina. Now, if seeing consisted in mere sensation,
we should perceive the impression of the object turned
upside down, because we receive it thus ; but in that case
we should perceive it as something within our eye, for we
should stop short at the sensation. In reality, however,
the Understanding steps in at once with its causal law, and
as it has received from sensation the datum of the direction in which the ray impinged upon the retina, it pursues
that direction retrogressively up to the cause on both
lines ; so that this time the crossing takes place in the opposite direction, and the cause presents itself upright as an
external object in Space, *i.e.* in the position in which it
originally sent forth its rays, not that in which they reached

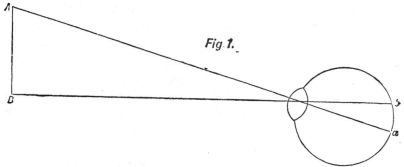

Fig. 1.

the retina (see fig. 1).—The purely intellectual nature of
this process, to the exclusion of all other, more especially of
physiological, explanations, may also be confirmed by the

fact, that if we put our heads between our legs, or lie down
on a hill head downwards, we nevertheless see objects in
their right position, and not upside down; although the
portion of the retina which is usually met by the lower part
of the object is then met by the upper: in fact, everything
is topsy turvy excepting the Understanding.

The *second* thing which the Understanding does in con-
verting sensation into perception, is to make a single perception out of a double sensation; for each eye in fact
receives its own separate impression from the object we are
looking at; each even in a slightly different direction:
nevertheless that object presents itself as a single one.
This can only take place in the Understanding, and the
process by which it is brought about is the following: Our
eyes are never quite parallel, excepting when we look at a
distant object, *i.e.* one which is more than 200 feet from
us.   At other times they are both directed towards the
object we are viewing, whereby they converge, so as to
make the lines proceeding from each eye to the exact point
of the object on which it is fixed, form an *angle,* called the
optic angle; the lines themselves are called *optic axes.*
Now, when the object lies straight before us, these lines
exactly impinge upon the centre of each retina, therefore
in two points which correspond exactly to each other in
each eye.   The Understanding, whose only business it is
to look for the *cause* of all things, at once recognises
the impression as coming from *a single* outside point,
although here the sensation is double, and attributes it to
one cause, which therefore presents itself as a single
object.   For all that is perceived by us, is perceived as a
cause—that is to say, as the cause of an effect we have
experienced, consequently *in the Understanding.*   As, nevertheless, we take in not only a single point, but a considerable surface of the object with both eyes, and yet perceive
it as a single object, it will be necessary to pursue this

explanation still further. All those parts of the object
which lie to one side of the vertex of the optic angle no
longer send their rays straight into the centre, but to the
side, of the retina in each eye; in both sides, however, to the
same, let us say the left, side. The points therefore
upon which these rays impinge, *correspond symmetrically to
each other*, as well as the centres—in other words, they are

Fig.2.

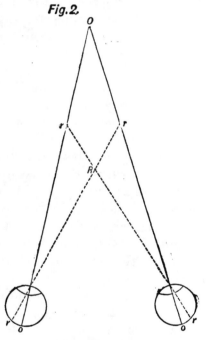

homonymous points. The Understanding soon learns to
know them, and accordingly extends the above-mentioned
rule of its causal perception to them also; consequently it
not only refers those rays which impinge upon the centre
of each retina, but those also which impinge upon all the
other symmetrically corresponding places in both retinas,
to a single radiant point in the object viewed : that is, it
sees all these points likewise as single, and the entire

object also. Now, it should be well observed, that in this process it is not the outer side of one retina which corresponds to the outer side of the other, and the inner to the inner of each, but the right side of one retina which corresponds to the right side of the other, and so forth ; so that this symmetrical correspondence must not be taken in a physiological, but in a geometrical sense. Numerous and very clear illustrations of this process, and of all the phenomena which are connected with it, are to be found in Robert Smith's "Optics," and partly also in Kästner's German translation (1755). I only give *one* (fig. 2), which, properly speaking, represents a special case, mentioned further on, but which may also serve to illustrate the whole, if we leave the point R out of question. According to this illustration, we invariably direct both eyes equally towards the object, in order that the symmetrically corresponding places on both retinas may catch the rays projected from the same points. Now, when we move our eyes upwards and downwards, to the sides, and in all directions, the point in the object which first impinged upon the central point of each, retina, strikes a different place every time, but in all cases one which, in each eye, corresponds to the place bearing the same name in the other eye. In examining (*perlustrare*) an object, we let our eyes glide backwards and forwards over it, in order to bring each point of it successively into contact with the centre of the retina, which sees most distinctly : we feel it all over with our eyes. It is therefore obvious that seeing singly with two eyes is in fact the same process as feeling a body with ten fingers, each of which receives a different impression, each moreover in a different direction : the totality of these impressions being nevertheless recognised by the Understanding as proceeding from *one* object, whose shape and size it accordingly apprehends and constructs in Space. This is why it is possible for a blind man to become

a sculptor, as was the case, for instance, with the famous
Joseph Kleinhaus, who died in Tyrol, 1853, having been a
sculptor from his fifth year.[1] For, no matter from what
cause it may have derived its data, perception is invariablv
an operation of the Understanding.

But just as a single ball seems to me double, if I touch
it with my fingers crossed—since my Understanding, at once
reverting to the cause and constructing it according to the
laws of Space, takes for granted that the fingers are in
their normal position and of course cannot do otherwise
than attribute two spherical surfaces, which come in contact
with the outer sides of the first and middle fingers, to two
different balls—just so also does an object seem double,
if my eyes, instead of converging symmetrically and en-
closing the optic angle at a single point of the object, each
view it at a different inclination—in other words, if I
squint. For the rays, which in this case emanate from *one*
point of the object, no longer impinge upon those symmetrically corresponding points in both retinas with which my
mind has grown familiar by long experience, but upon
other, quite different ones which, in a symmetrical position
of the eyes, could only be affected in this way by different

[1] The Frankfort "Konversationsblatt," July 22, 1853, gives the
following account of this sculptor :—" The blind sculptor, Joseph
Kleinhaus, died at Nauders, in Tyrol, on the 10th inst. Having lost
his eyesight through small-pox when he was five years old, he began to
amuse himself with carving and modelling, as a pastime. Prugg gave
him some instructions, and supplied him with models, and at the age of
twelve he carved a Christ in life-size. During a short stay in Nissl's
workshop at Fügen, his progress was so rapid, that, thanks to his good
capacities and talents, his fame as the blind sculptor soon spread far and
wide. His works are numerous and of various kinds. His Christs
alone, of which there are about four hundred, bear special witness to his
proficiency, particularly if his blindness is taken into consideration. He
sculptured many other objects besides, and, but two months ago, he
modelled a bust of the Emperor Franz Joseph of Austria which has
been sent to Vienna."

bodies ; I therefore now see *two* objects, precisely because perception takes place by means of, and within, the Understanding.—The same thing happens without squinting when, for instance, I look fixedly at the furthest of two objects placed at unequal distances before me, and complete the optic angle at it; for then the rays emanating from the nearer object do not impinge upon symmetrically corresponding places in both retinas, wherefore my Understanding attributes them to two objects, *i.e.* I see the nearer object double (see fig. 2, page 70). If, on the contrary, I complete the optic angle at the nearer object, by looking steadily at it, the further object appears double. It is easy to test this by holding a pencil two feet from the eyes, and looking alternately at it and at some other more distant object behind it.

But the finest thing of all is, that this experiment may quite well be reversed : so that, with two real objects straight before and close to us, and with our eyes wide open, we nevertheless see but *one*. This is the most striking proof that perception is a work of the Understanding and by no means contained in sensation. Let two cardboard tubes, about 8 inches long and $1\frac{1}{2}$ inches in diameter, be fastened parallel to one another, like those of a binocular telescope, and fix a shilling at the end of each tube. On applying our eyes to the opposite extremity and looking through the tubes, we shall see only *one* shilling surrounded by *one* tube. For in this case the eyes being forced into a completely parallel position, the rays emanating from the coins impinge exactly upon the centres of the two retinas and those points which immediately surround them, therefore upon places which correspond symmetrically to each other ; consequently the Understanding, taking for granted the usual convergent position of the optic axes when objects are near, admits but one object as the cause of the reflected rays. In other words, we see but one object; so direct is the act of causal apprehension in the Understanding.

We have not space enough here to refute one by one the physiological explanations of single vision which have been attempted; but their fallacy is shown by the following considerations:—

1°. If seeing single were dependent upon an organic connection, the corresponding points in both retinas, on which this phenomenon is shown to depend, would correspond *organically*, whereas they do so in a merely *geometrical* sense, as has already been said. For, organically speaking, the two inner and two outer corners of the eyes are those which correspond, and so it is with the other parts also; whereas for the purpose of single vision, it is the right side of the right retina which corresponds to the right side of the left retina, and so on, as the phenomena just described irrefutably show. It is also precisely on account of the intellectual character of the process, that only the most intelligent animals, such as the higher mammalia and birds of prey—more especially owls—have their eyes placed so as to enable them to direct both optic axes to the same point.

2°. The hypothesis of a confluence or partial intersection of the optic nerves before entering the brain, originated by Newton,[1] is false, simply because it would then be impossible to see double by squinting. Vesalius and Cæsalpinus besides have already brought forward anatomical instances in which subjects saw single, although neither fusion nor even contact of the optic nerves had taken place. A final argument against the hypothesis of a mixed impression is supplied by the fact, that on closing our right eye firmly and looking at the sun with our left, the bright image which persists for a time is always in the left, never in the right, eye: and *vice versa*.

[1] Newton, " Optics." Query 15.

The *third* process by which the Understanding converts sensation into perception, consists in constructing bodies out of the simple surfaces hitherto obtained—that is, in adding the third dimension. This it does by estimating the expansion of bodies in this third dimension in Space—which is known to the Understanding *à priori*—through Causality, according to the degree in which the eye is affected by the objects, and to the gradations of light and shade. In fact, although objects fill Space in all three dimensions, they can only produce an impression upon the eye with two; for the nature of that organ is such, that our sensation, in seeing, is merely planimetrical, not stereometrical. All that is stereometrical in our perception is added by the Understanding, which has for its sole data the direction whence the eye receives its impression, the limits of that impression, and the various gradations of light and dark: these data directly indicate their causes, and enable us to distinguish whether what we have before us is a disk or a ball. This mental process, like the preceding ones, takes place so immediately and with such rapidity, that we are conscious of nothing but the result. It is this which makes perspective drawing so difficult a problem, that it can only be solved by mathematics and has to be learnt; although all it has to do, is to represent the sensation of seeing as it presents itself to our Understanding as a datum for the third process: that is, visual sensation in its merely planimetrical extension, to the *two* dimensions of which extension, together with the said data in them, the Understanding forthwith adds the *third*, in contemplating a drawing as well as in contemplating reality. Perspective drawing is, in fact, a sort of writing which can be read as easily as printed type, but which few are able to write; precisely because our intellect, in perceiving, only apprehends effects with a view to constructing their causes, immediately losing sight of the former as soon as it has

discovered the latter. For instance, we instantly recognise
a chair, whatever position it may be in; while drawing a
chair in any position belongs to the art which abstracts
from this third process of the Understanding, in order to present the data alone for the spectator himself to complete.
In its narrowest acceptation, as we have already seen, this is
the art of drawing in perspective; in a more comprehensive
sense, it is the whole art of painting. A painting presents
us with outlines drawn according to the rules of perspective; lighter and darker places proportioned to the effect
of light and shade; finally patches of colouring, which
are determined as to quality and intensity by the teaching
of experience. This the spectator reads and interprets by
referring similar effects to their accustomed causes. The
painter's art consists in consciously retaining the data of
visual sensation in the artist's memory, as they are *before*
this third intellectual process; while we, who are not artists,
cast them aside without retaining them in our memory,
as soon as we have made use of them for the purpose
described above. We shall become still better acquainted
with this third intellectual process by now passing on to a
fourth, which, from its intimate connection with the third,
serves to elucidate it.

This *fourth* operation of the Understanding consists in
acquiring knowledge of the distance of objects from us:
it is this precisely which constitutes that third dimension
of which we have been speaking. Visual sensation, as we
have said, gives us the *direction* in which objects lie, but
not their *distance* from us: that is, not their *position*. It
is for the *Understanding* therefore to find out this distance; or, in other words, the distance must be inferred
from purely *causal* determinations. Now the most important of these is the *visual angle,* which objects subtend;
yet even this is quite ambiguous and unable to decide
anything by itself. It is like a word of double meaning:

the sense, in which it is to be understood, can only be
gathered from its connection with the rest. An object
subtending the same visual angle may in fact be small
and near, or large and far off; and it is only when we have
previously ascertained its size, that the visual angle enables
us to recognise its distance: and conversely, its size, when
its distance is known to us. Linear perspective is based
upon the fact that the visual angle diminishes as the distance increases, and its principles may here be easily deduced. As our sight ranges equally in all directions, we
see everything in reality as from the interior of a hollow
sphere, of which our eye occupies the centre. Now in the
first place, an infinite number of intersecting circles pass
through the centre of this sphere in all directions, and
the angles measured by the divisions of these circles are
the possible angles of vision. In the second place, the
sphere itself modifies its size according to the length of
radius we give to it; therefore we may also imagine it as
consisting of an infinity of concentric, transparent spheres.
As all radii diverge, these concentric spheres augment in
size in proportion to their distance from us, and the degrees of their sectional circles increase correspondingly:
therefore the true size of the objects which occupy them
likewise increases. Thus objects are larger or smaller according to the size of the spheres of which they occupy
similar portions—say 10°—while their visual angle remains unchanged in both cases, leaving it therefore un-
decided, whether the 10° occupied by a given object belong
to a sphere of 2 miles, or of 10 feet diameter. Conversely,
if the size of the object has been ascertained, the number
of degrees occupied by it will diminish in proportion to
the distance and the size of the sphere to which we refer
it, and all its outlines will contract in similar proportion.
From this ensues the fundamental law of all perspective;
for, as objects and the intervals between them must ne-

cessarily diminish in constant proportion to their distance
from us, all their outlines thereby contracting, the result
will be, that with increasing distance, what is above us
will descend, what is below us will ascend, and all that
lies at our sides will come nearer together. This pro-
gressive convergence, this linear perspective, no doubt
enables us to estimate distances, so far as we have before
us an uninterrupted succession of visibly connected objects;
but we are not able to do this by means of the visual
angle alone, for here the help of another datum is required
by the Understanding, to act, in a sense, as commentary
to the visual angle, by indicating more precisely the share
we are to attribute to distance in that angle. Now there
are four principal data of this kind, which I am about to
specify. Thanks to these data, even where there is no
linear perspective to guide us, if a man standing at a distance of 200 feet appears to me subtending a visual angle
twenty-four times smaller than if he were only 2 feet off,
I can nevertheless in most cases estimate his size correctly.
All this proves once more that perception is not only a thing
of the senses, but of the intellect also.—I will here add the
following special and interesting fact in corroboration of
what I have said about the basis of linear perspective as
well as about the intellectual nature of all perception.
When I have looked steadily at a coloured object with
sharply defined outlines—say a red cross—long enough
for the physiological image to form in my eye as a green
cross, the further the surface on to which I project it,
the larger it will appear to me: and *vice versa*. For the
image itself occupies an unvarying portion of my retina,
i.e. the portion originally affected by the red cross; therefore when referred outwards, or, in other words, recognised
as the effect of an external object, it forms an unchanging
visual angle, say of 2°. Now if, in this case, where all
commentary to the visual angle is wanting, I remove it to

a distant surface, with which I necessarily identify it as belonging to its effect, the cross will occupy 2° of a distant and therefore larger sphere, and is consequently large. If, on the other hand, I project the image on to a nearer object, it will occupy 2° of a smaller sphere, and is therefore small. The resulting perception is in both cases completely objective, quite like that of an external object; and as it proceeds from an entirely subjective reason (from the image having been excited in quite a different way), it thus confirms the intellectual character of all objective perception.—This phenomenon (which I distinctly remember to have been the first to notice, in 1815) forms the theme of an essay by Séguin, published in the "*Comptes rendus*" of the 2nd August, 1858, where it is served up as a new discovery, all sorts of absurd and distorted explanations of it being given. *Messieurs les illustres confrères* let pass no opportunity for heaping experiment upon experiment, the more complicated the better. *Expérience!* is their watchword; yet how rarely do we meet with any sound, genuine reflection upon the phenomena observed! *Expérience! expérience!* followed by twaddle.

To return to the subsidiary data which act as commentaries to a given visual angle, we find foremost among them the *mutationes oculi internæ*, by means of which the eye adapts its refractory apparatus to various distances by increasing and diminishing the refraction. In what these modifications consist, has not yet been clearly ascertained. They have been sought in the increased convexity, now of the *cornea*, now of the crystalline *lens;* but the latest theory seems to me the most probable one, according to which the lens is moved backwards for distant vision and forwards for near vision, lateral pressure, in the latter case, giving it increased protuberance; so that the process would exactly resemble the mechanism of an opera-glass.

Kepler, however, had, in the main, already expressed this theory, which may be found explained in A. Hueck's pamphlet, "Die Bewegung der Krystallinse," 1841. If we are not clearly conscious of these inner modifications of the eye, we have at any rate a certain feeling of them, and of this we immediately avail ourselves to estimate distances. As however these modifications are not available for the purposes of clear sight beyond the range of from about 7 inches to 16 feet, the Understanding is only able to apply this datum within those limits.

Beyond them, however, the second datum becomes available : that is to say, the *optic angle*, formed by the two optic axes, which we had occasion to explain when speaking of single vision. It is obvious that this optic angle becomes smaller, the further the object is removed : and *vice versa*. This different direction of the eyes, with respect to each other, does not take place without producing a slight sensation, of which we are nevertheless only in so far conscious as the Understanding makes use of it, as a datum, in estimating distances intuitively. By this datum we are not only enabled to cognize the distance, but the precise position of the object viewed, by means of the parallax of the eyes, which consists in each eye seeing the object in a slightly different direction ; so that if we close one eye, the object seems to move. Thus it is not easy to snuff a candle with one eye shut, because this datum is then wanting. But as the direction of the eyes becomes parallel as soon as the distance of the object reaches or exceeds 200 feet, and as the optic angle consequently then ceases to exist, this datum only holds good within the said distance.

Beyond it, the Understanding has recourse to *atmospheric perspective*, which indicates a greater distance by means of the increasing dimness of all colours, of the appearance of physical blue in front of all dark objects (according to Göthe's perfectly correct and true theory of colours), and also of the growing indistinctness of all outlines. In Italy, where the atmosphere is very transparent, this datum loses its power and is apt to mislead: Tivoli, for instance, seems to be very near when seen from Frascati. On the other hand, all objects appear larger in a mist, which is an abnormal exaggeration of the datum ; because our Understanding assumes them to be further from us.

Finally, there remains the estimation of distance by means of the size (known to us intuitively) of intervening objects, such as fields, woods, rivers, &c. &c. This mode of estimation is only applicable where there is uninterrupted succession : in other words, it can only be applied to terrestrial, not to celestial objects. Moreover, we have in general more practice in using it horizontally than vertically : a ball on the top of a tower 200 feet high appears much smaller to us than when lying on the ground 200 feet from us ; because, in the latter case, we estimate the distance more accurately. When we see human beings in such a way, that what lies between them and ourselves is in a great measure hidden from our sight, they always appear strikingly small.

The fact that our Understanding assumes everything it perceives in a horizontal direction to be farther off, therefore larger, than what is seen in a vertical direction, must partly be attributed to this last mode of estimating distances, inasmuch as it only holds good when applied horizontally and to terrestrial objects ; but partly also to our estimation of distances by atmospheric perspective, which is subject to similar conditions. This is why the moon seems so much larger on the horizon than at its zenith, although its visual angle accurately measured—that is, the image projected by it on to the eye—is not at all larger in one case than in the other ; and this also accounts for the flattened appearance of

the vault of the sky : that is to say, for its appearing to have
greater horizontal than vertical extension. Both phenomena therefore are purely intellectual or cerebral, not optical.
If it be objected, that even when at its zenith, the moon
occasionally has a hazy appearance without seeming to be
larger, we answer, that neither does it in that case appear
red; for its haziness proceeds from a greater density of
vapours, and is therefore of a different kind from that
which proceeds from atmospheric perspective. To this
may be added what I have already said : that we only
apply this mode of estimating distances in a horizontal,
not in a perpendicular, direction ; besides, in this case,
other correctives come into play. It is related of Saussure
that, when on the Mont Blanc, he saw so enormous a
moon rise, that, not recognising what it was, he fainted
with terror.

The properties of the telescope and magnifying glass,
on the other hand, depend upon a separate estimate
according to the visual angle alone : *i.e.*, that of size
by distance, and of distance by size; because here the
four other supplementary means of estimating distances
are excluded. The telescope in reality magnifies objects,
while it only seems to bring them nearer; because their
size being known to us empirically, we here account for
its apparent increase by a diminution of their distance
from us. A house seen through a telescope, for instance,
seems to be ten times nearer, not ten times larger, than
seen with the naked eye. The magnifying glass, on the
contrary, does not really magnify, but merely enables
us to bring the object nearer to our eyes than would
otherwise be possible ; so that it only appears as large
as it would at that distance even without the magnifying glass. In fact, we are prevented from seeing objects
distinctly at less than from eight to ten inches' distance
from our eyes, by the insufficient convexity of the ocular

lens and cornea; but if we increase the refraction by
substituting the convexity of the magnifying glass for
that of the lens and cornea, we then obtain a clear image
of objects even when they are as near as half an inch from
our eyes. Objects thus seen in close proximity to us and
in the size corresponding to that proximity, are transferred
by our Understanding to the distance at which we naturally
see distinctly, *i.e.* to about eight or ten inches from our
eyes, and we then estimate their magnitude according to
this distance and to the given visual angle.

I have entered thus fully into detail concerning all the
different processes by which seeing is accomplished, in
order to show clearly and irrefragably that the predomi-
nant factor in them is *the Understanding*, which, by con-
ceiving each change as an *effect* and referring that effect to
its *cause*, produces the cerebral phenomenon of the objective world on the basis of the *à priori* fundamental intuitions of Space and Time, for which it receives merely a
few data from the senses. And moreover the Understanding effects this exclusively by means of its own peculiar
form, the law of Causality; therefore quite directly and
intuitively, without any assistance whatever from reflection—that is, from abstract knowledge by means of conceptions and of language, which are the materials of *secondary*
knowledge, *i.e.* of *thought*, therefore of *Reason*.

That this knowledge through the Understanding is independent of Reason's assistance, is shown even by the
fact, that when, at any time, the Understanding attributes
a given effect to a wrong cause, actually perceiving that
cause, whereby *illusion* arises, our Reason, however clearly
it may recognise *in abstracto* the true state of the matter,
is nevertheless unable to assist the Understanding, and
the illusion persists undisturbed in spite of that better
knowledge. The above-mentioned phenomena of seeing
and feeling double, which result from an abnormal position

of the organs of touch and sight, are instances of such
illusions; likewise the apparently increased size of the
rising moon; the image which forms in the focus of a
concave mirror and exactly resembles a solid body floating
in space; the painted relievo which we take for real; the
apparent motion of a shore or bridge on which we are
standing, if a ship happens to pass along or beneath it; the
seeming proximity of very lofty mountains, owing to the
absence of atmospheric perspective, which is the result of
the purity of the air round their summits. In these and
in a multitude of similar cases, our Understanding takes
for granted the existence of the usual cause with which it is
conversant and forthwith perceives it, though our Reason
has arrived at the truth by a different road; for, the
knowledge of the Understanding being anterior to that of
the Reason, the intellect remains inaccessible to the teaching
of the Reason, and thus the *illusion*—that is, the deception of
the Understanding—remains immovable; albeit *error*—that
is, the deception of the Reason—is obviated.—That which
is correctly known by the Understanding is *reality*: that
which is correctly known by the Reason is *truth*, or in other
terms, a judgment having a sufficient reason; *illusion*
(that which is wrongly perceived) we oppose to *reality*:
error (that which is wrongly thought) to *truth*.

The purely formal part of empirical perception—that is,
Space, Time, and the law of Causality—is contained *à
priori* in the intellect; but this is not the case with the
application of this formal part to empirical data, which has
to be acquired by the Understanding through practice and
experience. Therefore new-born infants, though they no
doubt receive impressions of light and of colour, still do
not apprehend or indeed, strictly speaking, see objects.
The first weeks of their existence are rather passed in a
kind of stupor, from which they awaken by degrees when
their Understanding begins to apply its function to the

data supplied by the senses, especially those of touch and
of sight, whereby they gradually gain consciousness of the
objective world. This newly-arising consciousness may be
clearly recognised by the look of growing intelligence in
their eyes and a degree of intention in their movements,
especially in the smile with which they show for the first
time recognition of those who take care of them. They
may even be observed to make experiments for a time
with their sight and touch, in order to complete their
apprehension of objects by different lights, in different
directions and at different distances : thus pursuing a
silent, but serious course of study, till they have succeeded
in mastering all the intellectual operations in seeing which
have been described. The fact of this schooling can be
ascertained still more clearly through those who, being
born blind, have been operated upon late in life, since they
are able to give an account of their impressions. Chesel-
den's blind man [1] was not an isolated instance, and we
find in all similar cases the fact corroborated, that
those who obtain their sight late in life, no doubt, see
light, outlines, and colours, as soon as the operation is
over, but that they have no objective perception of objects
until their Understanding has learnt to apply its causal
law to data and to changes which are new to it. On first
beholding his room and the various objects in it, Chesel-
den's blind man did not distinguish one thing from
another ; he simply received the general impression of a
totality all in one piece, which he took for a smooth,
variegated surface. It never occurred to him to recognise
a number of detached objects, lying one behind the other
at different distances. With blind people of this sort, it
is by the sense of touch, to which objects are already
known, that they have to be introduced to the sense of

[1] See the original report in vol. 35 of the " Philosophical Transac-
tions" as to this case.

sight. In the beginning, the patient has no appreciation
whatever of distances and tries to lay hold of everything.
One, when he first saw his own house from outside, could
not conceive how so small a thing could contain so many
rooms. Another was highly delighted to find, some weeks
after the operation, that the engravings hanging on the
walls of his room represented a variety of objects. The
" Morgenblatt " of October 23rd, 1817, contains an account
of a youth who was born blind, and obtained his sight
at the age of seventeen. He had to learn intelligent
perception, for at first sight he did not even recognise
objects previously known to him through the sense of
touch. Every object had to be introduced to the sense of
sight by means of the sense of touch. As for the distances
of the objects he saw, he had no appreciation whatever of
them, and tried to lay hold indiscriminately of everything,
far or near.—Franz expresses himself as follows : [1]—

" A definite idea of distance, as well as of form and size, is only obtained by sight and touch, and by reflecting on the impressions made
on both senses; but for this purpose we must take into account the
muscular motion and voluntary locomotion of the individual.—Caspar
Hauser, in a detailed account of his own experience in this respect, states,
that upon his first liberation from confinement, whenever he looked through
the window upon external objects, such as the street, garden, &c., it appeared to him as if there were a shutter quite close to his eye, and covered
with confused colours of all kinds, in which he could recognise or distinguish nothing singly. He says farther, that he did not convince himself till
after some time during his walks out of doors, that what had at first
appeared to him as a shutter of various colours, as well as many other
objects, were in reality very different things; and that at length the
shutter disappeared, and he saw and recognised all things in their just
proportions. Persons born blind who obtain their sight by an operation in later years only, sometimes imagine that all objects touch their
eyes, and lie so near to them that they are afraid of stumbling against
them ; sometimes they leap towards the moon, supposing that they can

---

[1] Franz, " The Eye, a treatise on preserving this organ in a healthy
state and improving the sight." London, Churchill, 1839, pp. 34-36.

lay hold of it; at other times they run after the clouds moving along
the sky, in order to catch them, or commit other such extravagancies.
Since ideas are gained by reflection upon sensation, it is further necessary in all cases, in order that an accurate idea of objects may be
formed from the sense of sight, that the powers of the mind should be
unimpaired, and undisturbed in their exercise. A proof of this is
afforded in the instance related by Haslam,[1] of a boy who had no
defect of sight, but was weak in understanding, and who in his seventh
year was unable to estimate the distances of objects, especially as to
height; he would extend his hand frequently towards a nail on the
ceiling, or towards the moon, to catch it. It is therefore the judgment
which corrects and makes clear this idea, or perception of visible
objects."

The intellectual nature of perception as I have shown it,
is corroborated physiologically by Flourens [2] as follows :—

"Il faut faire une grand distinction entre les sens et l'intelligence.
L'ablation d'un tubercule détermine la perte de la *sensation*, du *sens* de
la vue; la rétine devient insensible, l'iris devient immobile. L'ablation
d'un lobe cérébral laisse la *sensation*, le *sens*, la *sensibilité* de la rétine,
la *mobilité* de l'iris; elle ne détruit que la *perception* seule. Dans un
cas, c'est un fait *sensorial;* et, dans l'autre, un fait *cérébral;* dans un
cas, c'est la perte du *sens;* dans l'autre, c'est la perte de la *perception.*
La distinction des perceptions et des sensations est encore un grand
résultat; et il est démontré aux yeux. Il y a deux moyens de faire
perdre la vision par l'encéphale : 1º par les tubercules, c'est la perte du
sens, de la sensation ; 2º par les lobes, c'est la perte de la perception, de
l'intelligence. La sensibilité n'est donc pas l'intelligence; penser n'est
donc pas sentir ; et voilà toute une philosophie renversée. L'idée n'est
donc pas la sensation ; et voilà encore une autre preuve du vice radical
de cette philosophie." And again, p. 77, under the heading : Sépara-
tion de la Sensibilité et de la Perception :—"Il y a une de mes expé-
rences qui sépare nettement la *sensibilité* de la *perception.* Quand
on enlève le *cerveau proprement dit* (*lobes* ou *hémisphères cérébraux*) à un
animal, l'animal perd la vue. Mais, par rapport a l'œil, rien n'est
changé : les objets continuent à se peindre sur la rétine; l'*iris* reste
contractile, le *nerf optique* sensible, parfaitement sensible. Et cepen-

---

[1] Haslam's "Observations on Madness and Melancholy," 2nd ed.
p. 192.
[2] Flourens, "De la vie et de l'Intelligence," 2nd edition, Paris,
Garnier Frères, 1852, p. 49.

88 THE FOURFOLD ROOT.   [CHAP. IV.

dant l'animal ne voit plus ; il n'y a plus *vision*, quoique tout ce qui est *sensation* subsiste ; il n'y a plus *vision*, parce qu'il n'y a plus *perception*. Le *percevoir*, et non le *sentir*, est donc le premier élément de l'*intelligence*. La *perception* est partie de l'*intelligence*, car elle se perd avec l'*intelligence*, et par l'ablation du même organe, les *lobes* ou *hémisphères cérébraux ;* et la *sensibilité* n'en est point partie, puisqu'elle subsiste après la perte de l'*intelligence* et l'ablation des *lobes* ou *hémisphères*."

The following famous verse of the ancient philosopher Epicharmus, proves that the ancients in general recognized the intellectual nature of perception : Νοῦς ὁρῇ καὶ νοῦς ἀκούει· τἆλλα κωφὰ καὶ τυφλά. (*Mens videt, mens audit ; cætera surda et cœca.*) [1] Plutarch in quoting this verse, adds : [2] ὡς τοῦ περὶ τὰ ὄμματα καὶ ὦτα πάθους, ἂν μὴ παρῇ τὸ φρονοῦν, αἴσθησιν οὐ ποιοῦντος (*quia affectio oculorum et aurium nullum affert sensum, intelligentia absente*). Shortly before too he says : Στράτωνος τοῦ φυσικοῦ λόγος ἐστίν, ἀπο δεικνύων ὡς οὐδ' αἰσθάνεσθαι τοπαράπαν ἄνευ τοῦ νοεῖν ὑπάρχει. (*Stratonis physici exstat ratiocinatio, qua " sine intelligentia sentiri omnino nihil posse" demonstrat.*) [3] Again shortly after he says : ὅθεν ἀνάγκη, πᾶσιν, οἷς τὸ αἰσθάνεσθαι, καὶ τὸ νοεῖν ὑπάρχειν, εἰ τῷ νοεῖν αἰσθάνεσθαι πεφύκαμεν (*quare necesse est, omnia, quæ sentiunt, etiam intelligere, siquidem intelligendo demum sentiamus*).[4] A second verse of Epicharmus might be connected with this, which is quoted by Diogenes Laertes (iii. 16) :

Εὔμαιε, τὸ σοφόν ἐστιν οὐ καθ' ἓν μόνον,
ἀλλ' ὅσα περ ζῇ, πάντα καὶ γνώμαν ἔχει.

[1] " It is the mind that sees and hears; all besides is deaf and blind." (Tr. Ad.)
[2] Plutarch, " De solert. animal." c. 3. " For the affection of our eyes and ears does not produce any perception, unless it be accompanied by thought." (Tr. Ad.)
[3] " Straton, the physicist, has proved that ' without thinking it is quite impossible to perceive.'" (Tr. Ad.)
[4] " Therefore it is necessary that all who perceive should also think, since we are so constituted as to perceive by means of thinking." (Tr. Ad.)

(*Eumaee, sapientia non uni tantum competit, sed quæcunque vivunt etiam intellectum habent.*) Porphyry likewise endea-vours to show at length that all animals have under-standing.[1]

Now, that it should be so, follows necessarily from the intellectual character of perception. All animals, even down to the very lowest, must have Understanding—that is, knowledge of the causal law, although they have it in very different degrees of delicacy and of clearness; at any rate they must have as much of it as is required for percep-tion by their senses; for sensation without Understanding would be not only a useless, but a cruel gift of Nature. No one, who has himself any intelligence, can doubt the existence of it in the higher animals. But at times it even becomes undeniably evident that their knowledge of causality is actually *à priori*, and that it does not arise from the habit of seeing one thing follow upon another. A very young puppy will not, for instance, jump off a table, because he foresees what would be the consequence. Not long ago I had some large curtains put up at my bed-room window, which reached down to the floor, and were drawn aside from the centre by means of a string. The first morning they were opened I was surprised to see my dog, a very intelligent poodle, standing quite perplexed, and looking upwards and sidewards for the cause of the phenomenon : that is, he was seeking for the change which he knew *à priori* must have taken place. Next day the same thing happened again.—But even the lowest animals have perception—consequently Understanding—down to the aquatic polypus, which has no distinct organs of sensa-tion, yet wanders from leaf to leaf on its waterplant, while clinging to it with its feelers, in search of more light.

Nor is there, indeed, any difference, beyond that of

[1] Porph. " De abstinentia," iii. 21.

degree, between this lowest Understanding and that of man, which we however distinctly separate from his Reason. The intermediate gradations are occupied by the various series of animals, among which the highest, such as the monkey, the elephant, the dog, astonish us often by their intelligence. But in every case the business of the Understanding is invariably to apprehend directly causal relations : first, as we have seen, those between our own body and other bodies, whence proceeds objective perception; then those between these objectively perceived bodies among themselves, and here, as has been shown in § 20, the causal relation manifests itself in three forms—as cause, as stimulus, and as motive. All movement in the world takes place according to these three forms of the causal relation, and through them alone does the intellect comprehend it. Now, if, of these three, *causes*, in the narrowest sense of the word, happen to be the object of invesgation for the Understanding, it will produce Astronomy, Mechanics, Physics, Chemistry, and will invent machines for good and for evil ; but in all cases a direct, intuitive apprehension of the causal connection will in the last resort lie at the bottom of all its discoveries. For the sole form and function of the Understanding is this apprehension, and not by any means the complicated machinery of Kant's twelve Categories, the nullity of which I have proved.— (All comprehension is a direct, consequently intuitive, apprehension of the causal connection; although this has to be reduced at once to abstract conceptions in order to be fixed. To calculate therefore, is not to understand, and, in itself, calculation conveys no comprehension of things. Calculation deals exclusively with abstract conceptions of magnitudes, whose mutual relations it determines. By it we never attain the slightest comprehension of a physical process, for this requires *intuitive* comprehension of space-relations, by means of which causes take effect.

Calculations have merely practical, not theoretical, value.. It may even be said that *where calculation begins, comprehension ceases ;* for a brain occupied with numbers is, as long as it calculates, entirely estranged from the causal connection in physical processes, being engrossed in purely abstract, numerical conceptions. The result, however, only shows us *how much,* never *what.* " *L'expérience et le calcul,*" those watchwords of French physicists, are not therefore by any means adequate [for thorough insight].)— If, again, *stimuli* are the guides of the Understanding, it will produce Physiology of Plants and Animals, Therapeutics, and Toxicology. Finally, if it devotes itself to the study of *motives,* the Understanding will use them, on the one hand, theoretically, to guide it in producing works on Morality, Jurisprudence, History, Politics, and even Dramatic and Epic Poetry; on the other hand, practically, either merely to train animals, or for the higher purpose of making human beings dance to its music, when once it has succeeded in discovering which particular wire has to be pulled in order to move each puppet at its pleasure. Now, with reference to the function which effects this, it is quite immaterial whether the intellect turns gravitation ingeniously to account, and makes it serve its purpose by stepping in just at the right time, or whether it brings the collective or the individual propensities of men into play for its own ends. In its practical application we call the Understanding *shrewdness* or, when used to outwit others, *cunning ;* when its aims are very insignificant, it is called *slyness* and, if combined with injury to others, *craftiness.* In its purely theoretical application, we call it simply *Understanding,* the higher degrees of which are named *acumen, sagacity, discernment, penetration,* while its lower degrees are termed *dulness, stupidity, silliness,* &c. &c. These widely differing degrees of sharpness are innate, and cannot be acquired ; although, as I have already shown,

even in the earliest stages of the application of the Understanding, *i.e.* in empirical perception, practice and knowledge of the material to which it is applied, are needed.
Every simpleton has Reason—give him the premisses, and
he will draw the conclusion; whereas *primary*, consequently intuitive, knowledge is supplied by the Understanding: herein lies the difference. The pith of every
great discovery, of every plan having universal historical
importance, is accordingly the product of a happy moment
in which, by a favourable coincidence of outer and inner
circumstances, some complicated causal series, some hidden
causes of phenomena which had been seen thousands of
times before, or some obscure, untrodden paths, suddenly
reveal themselves to the intellect.–

By the preceding explanations of the processes in seeing
and feeling, I have incontestably shown that empirical perception is essentially the work of *the Understanding*, for
which the material only is supplied by the senses in sensation—and a poor material it is, on the whole; so that *the
Understanding* is, in fact, the artist, while the senses are
but the under-workmen who hand it the materials. But
the process consists throughout in referring from given
effects to their causes, which by this process are enabled to
present themselves as objects in Space. The very fact that
we presuppose Causality in this process, proves precisely
that this law must have been supplied by the Understanding itself; for it could never have found its way into
the intellect from outside. It is indeed the first condition
of all empirical perception; but this again is the form in
which all external experience presents itself to us; how
then can this law of Causality be derived from experience,
when it is itself essentially presupposed by experience?—It
was just because of the utter impossibility of this, and
because Locke's philosophy had put an end to all *à priority*,
that Hume denied the whole reality of the conception of

Causality. He had besides already mentioned two false·
hypotheses in the seventh section of his "Inquiry concerning
the Human Understanding," which recently have again been.
advanced : the one, that the effect of the will upon the·
members of our body ; the other, that the resistance·
opposed to our pressure by outward objects, is the origin;
and prototype of the conception of Causality. Hume refutes.
both in his own way and according to his own order of.
ideas. I argue as follows. There is no causal connection..
whatever between acts of the will and actions of the body ;·
on the contrary, both are immediately one and the same
thing, only perceived in a double aspect—that is, on the·
one hand, in our self-consciousness, or inner sense, as acts·
of the will; on the other, simultaneously in exterior,.
spacial brain-perception, as actions of the body.[1] The·
second hypothesis is false, first because, as I have already
shown at length, a mere sensation of touch does not yet
give any objective perception whatever, let alone the con-·
ception of Causality, which never can arise from the feeling·
of an impeded muscular effort : besides impediments of this.
kind often occur without any external cause ; secondly,.
because our pressing against an external object necessarily·
has a motive, and this already presupposes apprehension of·
that object, which again presupposes knowledge of Cau-·
sality.—But the only means of radically proving the con-·
ception of Causality to be independent of all experience was
by showing, as I have done, that the whole possibility of·
experience is conditioned by the conception of Causality..
In § 23 I intend to show that Kant's proof, propounded
with a similar intent, is false.

This is also the proper place for drawing attention to the·

[1] Compare "Die Welt a. W. u. V." 3rd edition, vol. ii. p. 41.
[The 3rd edition of "Die Welt a. W. u. V." contains at this place a·
supplement which is wanting in the 2nd edition, vol. ii. p. 38.—Note by·
the Editor of the 3rd edition.]

fact, that Kant either did not clearly recognise in empirical perception the mediation of the causal law—which law is known to us before all experience—or that he intentionally evaded mentioning it, because it did not suit his purpose. In the " Critique of Pure Reason," for instance, the relation between causality and perception is not treated in the " Doctrine of Elements," but in the chapter on the " Paralogisms of Pure Reason," where one would hardly expect to find it; moreover it appears in his " Critique of the Fourth Paralogism of Transcendental Psychology," and only in the first edition.[1] The very fact that this place should have been assigned to it, shows that in considering this relation, he always had the transition from the phenomenon to the thing in itself exclusively in view, but not the genesis of perception itself. Here accordingly he says that the existence of a real external object is not given directly in perception, but can be added to it in thought and thus inferred. In Kant's eyes, however, he who does this is a Transcendental Realist, and consequently on a wrong road. For by his " outward object " Kant here means the thing in itself. The Transcendental Idealist, on the contrary, stops short at the perception of something empirically real—that is, of something existing outside us in Space—without needing the inference of a cause to give it reality. For *perception*, according to Kant, is quite directly accomplished without any assistance from the causal nexus, and consequently from the Understanding: he simply identifies perception with sensation. This we find confirmed in the passage which begins, " With reference to the reality of external objects, I need as little trust to inference," &c. &c.[2] and again in the sentence commencing with " Now we may well

---

[1] Kant, " Krit. d. r. V." 1st edition, p. 367 *sqq.* (English translation by M. Müller, p. 318 *sqq.*)

[2] Kant, " Krit. d. r. Vern." 1st edition, p. 371. (English translation, by M. Müller, p. 322.)

admit," &c. &c.[1]   It is quite clear from these passages that perception of external things in Space, according to Kant, precedes all application of the causal law, therefore that the causal law does not belong to perception as an element and condition of it: for him, mere sensation is identical with perception.   Only in as far as we ask what may, in a *transcendental* sense, exist *outside of us*: that is, when we ask for the thing in itself, is Causality mentioned as connected with perception.   Moreover Kant admits the existence, nay, the mere possibility, of causality only in reflection: that is, in abstract, distinct knowledge by means of conceptions; therefore he has no suspicion that its application is *anterior to all reflection*, which is nevertheless evidently the case, especially in empirical, sensuous perception which, as I have proved irrefragably in the preceding analysis, could never take place otherwise.   Kant is therefore obliged to leave the genesis of empirical perception unexplained.   With him it is a mere matter of the senses, given as it were in a miraculous way: that is, it coincides with sensation.   I should very much like my reflective readers to refer to the passages I have indicated in Kant's work, in order to convince themselves of the far greater accuracy of my view of the whole process and connection.   Kant's extremely erroneous view has held its ground till now in philosophical literature, simply because no one ventured to attack it; therefore I have found it necessary to clear the way in order to throw light upon the mechanism of our knowledge.

Kant's fundamental idealistic position loses nothing whatever, nay, it even gains by this rectification of mine, in as far as, with me, the necessity of the causal law is absorbed and extinguished in empirical perception as its product and cannot therefore be invoked in behalf of an

---

[1] Kant, "Krit. d. r. Vern." 1st edition, p. 372. (English translation, p. 323.)

entirely transcendent question as to the thing in itself.
On referring to my theory above concerning empirical perception, we find that its first datum, sensation, is absolutely
subjective, being a process within the organism, because it
takes place beneath the skin. Locke has completely and
exhaustively proved, that the feelings of our senses, even
admitting them to be roused by external causes, cannot
have any resemblance whatever to the qualities of those
causes. Sugar, for instance, bears no resemblance at all to
sweetness, nor a rose to redness. But that they should
need an external cause at all, is based upon a law whose
origin lies demonstrably within us, in our brain; therefore
this necessity is not less subjective than the sensations
themselves. Nay, even *Time*—that primary condition
of every possible *change*, therefore also of the change
which first permits the application of the causal law—and
not less *Space*—which alone renders the externalisation
of causes possible, after which they present themselves
to us as objects—even Time and Space, we say, are subjective forms of the intellect, as Kant has conclusively
proved. Accordingly we find all the elements of empirical perception lying within us, and nothing contained
in them which can give us reliable indications as to anything differing absolutely from ourselves, anything in
itself.—But this is not all. What we think under the conception *matter*, is the residue which remains over after
bodies have been divested of their shape and of all their
specific qualities: a residue, which precisely on that account
must be identical in all bodies. Now these shapes and
qualities which have been abstracted by us, are nothing
but the peculiar, specially defined *way in which these bodies
act*, which constitutes precisely their difference. If therefore we leave these shapes and qualities out of consideration, there remains nothing but *mere activity in general*,
pure action as such, Causality itself, objectively thought—

that is, the reflection of our own Understanding, the externalised image of its sole function; and Matter is throughout pure Causality, its essence is Action in general.[1] This is why pure Matter cannot be perceived, but can only be thought : it is a something we add to every reality, as its basis, in thinking it. For pure Causality, mere action, without any defined mode of action, cannot become perceptible, therefore it cannot come within any experience.—Thus Matter is only the objective correlate to pure Understanding; for it is Causality in general, and nothing else : just as the Understanding itself is direct knowledge of cause and effect, and nothing else. Now this again is precisely why the law of causality is not applicable to Matter itself : that is to say, Matter has neither beginning nor end, but is and remains permanent. For as, on the one hand, Causality is the indispensable condition of all alternation in the accidents (forms and qualities) of Matter, *i.e.* of all passage in and out of being ; but as, on the other hand, Matter s pure Causality itself, as such, objectively viewed : it is unable to exercise its own power upon itself, just as the eye can see everything but itself. " Substance " and Matte1 being moreover identical, we may call *Substance, action* viewed *in abstracto* : *Accidents*, particular modes of action, action *in concreto*.—Now these are the results to which true, *i.e.* transcendental, Idealism leads. In my chief work I have shown that the thing in itself—*i.e.* whatever, on the whole, exists independently of our representation—cannot be got at by way of representation, but that, to reach it, we must follow quite a different path, leading through the inside of things, which lets us into the citadel, as it were, by treachery.—

But it would be downright chicanery, nothing else, to

[1] Compare " Die Welt a. W. u. V." 2nd edition ; vol. i. sect. 4, p. 9 ; and vol. ii. pp. 48, 49 (3rd edition, vol. i. p. 10; vol. ii. p. 52). English translation, vol. i. pp. 9-10; vol. ii. p. 218.

try and compare, let alone identify, such an honest, deep, thorough analysis of empirical perception as the one I have just given, which proves all the elements of perception to be subjective, with Fichte's algebraic equations of the *Ego* and the *Non-Ego;* with his sophistical pseudo-demonstrations, which in order to be able to deceive his readers had to be clothed in the obscure, not to say absurd, language adopted by him ; with his explanations of the way in which the *Ego* spins the *Non-Ego* out of itself ; in short, with all the buffoonery of scientific emptiness.[1] Besides, I protest altogether against any community with this Fichte, as Kant publicly and emphatically did in a notice *ad hoc* in the "Jenaer Litteratur Zeitung." [2] Hegelians and similar ignoramuses may continue to hold forth to their heart's content upon Kant-Fichteian philosophy : there exists a Kantian philosophy and a Fichteian hocus-pocus,—this is the true state of the case, and will remain so, in spite of those who delight in extolling what is bad and in decrying what is good, and of these Germany possesses a larger number than any other country.

§. 22. *Of the Immediate Object.*

Thus it is from the sensations of our body that we receive the data for the very first application of the causal law, and it is precisely by that application that the perception of this class of objects arises. They therefore have their essence and existence solely in virtue of the intellectual function thus coming into play, and of its exercise.

---

[1] *Wissenschaftsleere* (literally, *emptiness of science*), a pun of Schopenhauer's on the title of Fichte's *Wissenschaftslehre* (*doctrine of science*), which cannot be rendered in English. (Tr.'s Note.)

[2] Kant, "Erklärung über Fichte's Wissenschaftslehre." See the "Intelligenzblatt" of the Jena Literary Gazette (1799), No. 109.

Now, as far as it is the starting-point, *i.e.* the mediator, for our perception of all other objects, I have called the bodily organism, in the first edition of the present work, the *Immediate Object;* this, however, must not be taken in a strictly literal sense. For although our bodily sensations are all apprehended directly, still this immediate apprehension does not yet make our body itself perceptible to us as an object; on the contrary, up to this point all remains subjective, that is to say, sensation. From this sensation certainly proceeds the perception of all other objects as the causes of such sensations, and these causes then present themselves to us as objects; but it is not so with the body itself, which only supplies sensations to consciousness. It is only *indirectly* that we know even this body objectively, *i.e.* as an object, by its presenting itself, like all other objects, as the recognised cause of a subjectively given effect—and precisely on this account *objectively*—in our Understanding, or brain (which is the same). Now this can only take place when its own senses are acted upon by its parts : for instance, when the body is seen by the eye, or felt by the hand, &c., upon which data the brain (or understanding) forthwith constructs it as to shape and quality in space.—The immediate presence in our consciousness of representations belonging to this class, depends therefore upon the position assigned to them in the causal chain—by which all things are *connected*—relatively to the body (for the time being) of the Subject —by which (the Subject) all things are *known*.

§. 23. *Arguments against Kant's Proof of the à priority of the conception of Causality.*

One of the chief objects of the "Critique of Pure Reason" is to show the universal validity, for all experience, of the causal law, its *à priority*, and, as a necessary

consequence of this, its restriction to possible experience.
Nevertheless, I cannot assent to the proof there given of
the *à priority* of the principle, which is substantially
this:—" The *synthesis* of the manifold by the imagination, which is necessary for all empirical knowledge,
gives succession, but not yet determinate succession :
that is, it leaves undetermined which of two states perceived was the first, not only in my imagination, but in the
object itself. But definite order in this succession—
through which alone what we perceive becomes experience,
or, in other words, authorizes us to form objectively valid
judgments—is first brought into it by the purely intellectual conception of cause and effect. Thus the principle
of causal relation is the condition which renders experience
possible, and, as such, it is given us *à priori.*" [1]

According to this, the order in which changes succeed
each other in real objects becomes known to us as objective only by their causality. This assertion Kant repeats
and explains in the "Critique of Pure Reason," especially
in his "Second Analogy of Experience," [2] and again at the
conclusion of his "Third Analogy," and I request every
one who desires to understand what I am now about to
say, to read these passages. In them he affirms everywhere that *the objectivity of the succession of representations*—which he defines as their correspondence with the
succession of real objects—is only known through the
rule by which they follow upon one another: that is,
through the law of causality ; that my mere apprehension
consequently leaves the objective relation between phenomena following one another quite undetermined : since

[1] Kant, " Krit. d. r. Vern." 1st edition, p. 201 ; 5th edition, p, 246.
(English translation by M. Müller, p. 176.) This is, however, not a
literal quotation. (Tr.'s note.)

[2] *Ibid.* p. 189 of the 1st edition; more fully, p. 232 of the 5th
edition. (English translation by M. Müller, p. 166.)

I merely apprehend the succession of my own representations, but the succession in my apprehension does not
authorize me to form any judgment whatever as to the
succession in the object, unless that judgment be based
upon causality; and since, besides, I might invert the order
in which these perceptions follow each other in my apprehension, there being nothing which determines them as
objective. To illustrate this assertion, Kant brings forward
the instance of a house, whose parts we may consider in any
order we like, from top to bottom, or from bottom to top;
the determination of succession being in this case purely
subjective and not founded upon an object, because it
depends upon our pleasure. In opposition to this instance,
he brings forward the perception of a ship sailing down a
river, which we see successively lower and lower down the
stream, which perception of the successively varying positions of the ship cannot be changed by the looker-on. In
this latter case, therefore, he derives the subjective following in his own apprehension from the objective following
in the phenomenon, and on this account he calls it an
event. Now I maintain, on the contrary, that *there is no
difference at all between these two cases, that both are events,*
and that our knowledge of both is objective : that is to say,
it is knowledge of changes in real objects recognized as
such by the Subject. *Both are changes of relative position
in two bodies.* In the first case, one of these bodies is a
part of the observer's own organism, the eye, and the other
is the house, with respect to the different parts of which
the eye successively alters its position. In the second, it
is the ship which alters its position towards the stream ;
therefore the change occurs between two bodies. Both are
events, the only difference being that, in the first, the
change has its starting-point in the observer's own body,
from whose sensations undoubtedly all his perceptions
originally proceed, but which is nevertheless an object

among objects, and in consequence obeys the laws of the objective, material world. For the observer, as a purely cognising individual, any movement of his body is simply an empirically perceived fact. It would be just as possible in the second as in the first instance, to invert the order of succession in the change, were it as easy for the observer to move the ship up the stream as to alter the direction of his own eyes. For Kant infers the successive perception of different parts of the house to be neither objective nor an event, because it depends upon his own will. But the movement of his eyes in the direction from roof to basement is one event, and in the direction from basement to roof another event, just as much as the sailing of the ship. There is no difference whatever here, nor is there any difference either, as to their being or not being events, between my passing a troop of soldiers and their passing me. If we fix our eyes on a ship sailing close by the shore on which we are standing, it soon seems as if it were the ship that stood still and the shore that moved. Now, in this instance we are mistaken, it is true, as to the cause of the relative change of position, since we attribute it to a wrong cause ; the real succession in the relative positions of our body towards the ship is nevertheless quite rightly and objectively recognised by us. Even Kant himself would not have believed that there was any difference, had he borne in mind that his own body was an object among objects, and that the succession in his empirical perceptions depended upon the succession of the impressions received from other objects by his body, and was therefore an objective succession : that is to say, one which takes place among objects *directly* (if not indirectly) and independently of the will of the Subject, and which may therefore be quite well recognised without any causal connection between the objects acting successively on his body.

Kant says, Time cannot be perceived; therefore no succession of representations can be empirically perceived as
objective: *i.e.* can be distinguished as changes in phenomena from the changes of mere subjective representations.
The causal law, being a rule according to which states
follow one another, is the only means by which the objectivity of a change can be known. Now, the result of
his assertion would be, that no succession in Time could
be perceived by us as objective, excepting that of cause
and effect, and that every other succession of phenomena
we perceive, would only be determined so, and not otherwise, by our own will. In contradiction to all this I must
adduce the fact, that it is quite possible for phenomena to
follow upon one another without *following from* one another.
Nor is the law of causality by any means prejudiced by
this; for it remains certain that each change is the effect
of another change, this being firmly established *à priori;*
only each change not only follows upon the single one
which is its cause, but upon all the other changes which
occur simultaneously with that cause, and with which that
cause stands in no causal connection whatever. It is not
perceived by me exactly in the regular order of causal
succession, but in quite a different order, which is, however, no less objective on that account, and which differs
widely from any subjective succession depending on my
caprice, such as, for instance, the pictures of my imagination. The succession, in Time, of events which stand in
no causal connection with each other is precisely what we
call *contingency.*[1] Just as I am leaving my house, a tile
happens to fall from the roof which strikes me; now, there
is no causal connection whatever between my going out and

[1] In German *Zufall*, a word derived from the *Zusammenfallen* (falling
together), *Zusammentreffen* (meeting together), or coinciding of what is
unconnected, just as τὸ συμβεβηκός from συμβαίνειν. (Compare Aristotle, " Anal. post.," i. 4.)

the falling of the tile ; yet the order of their succession—
that is, that my going out preceded the falling of the tile
—is objectively determined in my apprehension, not subjectively by my will, by which that order would otherwise
have most likely been inverted. The order in which tones
follow each other in a musical composition is likewise
objectively determined, not subjectively by me, the lis-
tener; yet who would think of asserting that musical
tones follow one another according to the law of cause and
effect? Even the succession of day and night is undoubtedly known to us as an objective one, but we as
certainly do not look upon them as causes and effects of
one another; and as to their common cause, the whole
world was in error till Copernicus came; yet the correct
knowledge of their succession was not in the least disturbed by that error. Hume's hypothesis, by the way,
also finds its refutation through this; since the following
of day and night upon each other—the most ancient of
all successions and the one least liable to exception—has
never yet misled anyone into taking them for cause and
effect of each other.

Elsewhere Kant asserts, that a representation only shows
reality (which, I conclude, means that it is distinguished
from a mere mental image) by our recognising its necessary
connection with other representations subject to rule (the
causal law) and its place in a determined order of the
time-relations of our representations. But of how few
representations are we able to know the place assigned to
them by the law of causality in the chain of causes and
effects! Yet we are never embarrassed to distinguish objective from subjective representations: real, from imaginary objects. When asleep, we are unable to make this
distinction, for our brain is then isolated from the peri-
pherical nervous system, and thereby from external influences. In our dreams therefore, we take imaginary for

real things, and it is only when we awaken : that is, when our nervous sensibility, and through this the outer world, once more comes within our consciousness, that we become aware of our mistake ; still, even in our dreams, so long as they last, the causal law holds good, only an impossible material is often substituted for the usual one. We might almost think that Kant was influenced by Leibnitz in writing the passage we have quoted, however much he differs from him in all the rest of his philosophy ; especially if we consider that Leibnitz expresses precisely similar views, when, for instance, he says : " La vérité des choses sensibles ne consiste que dans la liaison des phéno-mènes, qui doit avoir sa raison, et c'est ce qui les distingue des songes. — — — — Le vrai Critérion, en matière des objets des sens, est la liaison des phénomènes, qui garantit les vérités de fait, à l'égard des choses sensibles hors de nous."[1]

It is clear that in proving the *à priority* and the ne-cessity of the causal law by the fact that the objective succession of changes is known to us only by means of that law, and that, in so far, causality is a condition for all experience, Kant fell into a very singular error, and one which is indeed so palpable, that the only way we can account for it is, by supposing him to have become so absorbed in the *à priori* part of our knowledge, that he lost sight of what would have been evident to anyone else. The only correct demonstration of the *à priority* of the causal law is given by me in § 21 of the present work. That *à priority* finds its confirmation every moment in the infallible security with which we expect experience to tally with the causal law : that is to say, in the apodeictic cer-tainty we ascribe to it, a certainty which differs from every other founded on induction—the certainty, for in-

[1] Leibnitz, " Nouveaux Essais sur l'Entendement," lib. iv. ch. ii. sect. 14.

stance, of empirically known laws of Nature—in that we can conceive no exception to the causal law anywhere within the world of experience. We can, for instance, *conceive* that in an exceptional case the law of gravitation might cease to act, but not that this could happen without a cause.

Kant and Hume have fallen into opposite errors in their proofs. Hume asserts that all *consequence* is mere *sequence;* whereas Kant affirms that all *sequence* must necessarily be *consequence.* Pure Understanding, it is true, can only conceive *consequence* (causal result), and is no more able to conceive mere *sequence* than to conceive the difference between right and left, which, like sequence, is only to be grasped by means of pure Sensibility. Empirical knowledge of the following of events in Time is, indeed, just as possible as empirical knowledge of juxtaposition of things in Space (this Kant denies elsewhere), but *the way in which* things follow *upon* one another in general in Time can no more be explained, than the way in which one thing follows *from* another (as the effect of a cause) : the former knowledge is given and conditioned by pure Sensibility ; the latter, by pure Understanding. But in asserting that knowledge of the objective succession of phenomena can only be attained by means of the causal law, Kant commits the same error with which he reproaches Leibnitz : [1] that of "intellectualising the forms of Sensibility."—My view of succession is the following one. We derive our knowledge of the bare *possibility* of succession from the form of Time, which belongs to pure Sensibility. The succession of real objects, whose form is precisely Time, we know empirically, consequently as *actual.* But it is through the Understanding alone, by means of Causality, that we gain knowledge of the *necessity* of a succession of

---

[1] Kant, " Kritik d. r. Vern." 1st edition, p. 275 ; 5th edition, p. 331. (English translation by M. Müller, p. 236.)

two states: that is, of a change; and even the fact that we are able to conceive the necessity of a succession at all, proves already that the causal law is not known to us empirically, but given us *à priori.* The Principle of Sufficient Reason is the general expression for the fundamental form of the necessary connection between all our objects, *i.e.* representations, which lies in the innermost depths of our cognitive faculty : it is the form common to all representations, and the only source of the conception of *necessity,* which contains absolutely nothing else in it and no other import, than that of the following of the consequence, when its reason has been established. Now, the reason why this principle determines the order of succession in Time in the class of representations we are now investigating, in which it figures as the law of causality, is, that Time is the form of these representations, therefore the necessary connection appears here as the rule of succession. In other forms of the principle of sufficient reason, the necessary connection it always demands will appear under quite different forms from that of Time, therefore not as succession ; still it always retains the character of a necessary connection, by which the identity of the principle under all its forms, or rather the unity of the root of all the laws of which that principle is the common expression, reveals itself.

If Kant's assertion were correct, which I dispute, our only way of knowing the reality of succession would be through its necessity; but this would presuppose an Understanding that embraced all the series of causes and effects at once, consequently an omniscient Understanding. Kant has burdened the Understanding with an impossibility, merely in order to have less need of Sensibility.

How can we reconcile Kant's assertion that our only means of knowing the objective reality of succession is by the necessity with which effect follows cause, with his other assertion[1] that succession in Time is our only empirical criterion for determining which of two states is cause, and which effect. Who does not see the most obvious circle here?

If we knew objectiveness of succession through Causality, we should never be able to think it otherwise than as Causality, and then it would be nothing else than Causality. F᷒r, if it were anything else, it would have other distinctive signs by which to be recognised; now this is just what Kant denies. Accordingly, if Kant were right, we could not say : "This state is the effect of that one, wherefore it follows it;" for following and being an effect, would be one and the same thing, and this proposition a tautology. Besides, if we do away with all distinction between following *upon* and following *from*, we once more yield the point to Hume, who declared all consequence to be mere sequence and therefore denied that distinction likewise.

Kant's proof would, consequently, be reduced to this : that, empirically, we only know *actuality* of succession; but as besides we recognise *necessity* of succession in certain series of occurrences, and even know before all experience that every possible occurrence must have a fixed place in some one of these series, the reality and the *à priority* of the causal law follow as a matter of course, the only correct proof of the latter being the one I have given in § 21 of this work.

Parallel with the Kantian theory : that the causal nexus alone renders objective succession and our knowledge of it possible, there runs another : that coexistence and our knowledge of it are only possible through reciprocity. In the "Critique of Pure Reason" they are presented under

[1] Kant, "Krit. d. r. Vern." vol. i. p. 203 of the 1st edition; p. 249 of the 5th edition. (English translation by M. Müller, p. 178.)

the title: " Third Analogy of Experience." Here Kant
goes so far as to say that " the co-existence of phenomena,
which exercise no reciprocal action on one another, but are
separated by a perfectly empty space, could never become
an object of possible perception " [1] (which, by the way,
would be a proof à priori that there is no empty space
between the fixed stars), and that " the light which *plays*
between our eyes and celestial bodies "—an expression
conveying surreptitiously the thought, that this starlight
not only acts upon our eyes, but is acted upon by them
also—" produces an intercommunity between us and them,
and proves the co-existence of the latter." Now, even
empirically, this last assertion is false; since the sight of a
fixed star by no means proves its coexistence simultaneously with its spectator, but, at most, its existence
some years, nay even some centuries before. Besides, this
second Kantian theory stands and falls with the first,
only it is far more easily detected; and the nullity of
the whole conception of reciprocity has been shown in
§ 20.

The arguments I have brought forward against Kant's
proof may be compared with two previous attacks made on
it by Feder,[2] and by G. E. Schulze.[3]

Not without considerable hesitation did I thus venture
(in 1813) to attack a theory which had been universally
received as a demonstrated truth, is repeated even now in the
latest publications,[4] and forms a chief point in the doctrine
of one for whose profound wisdom I have the greatest
reverence and admiration; one to whom, indeed, I owe so

---

[1] Kant, " Krit. d. r. Vern." pp. 212 and 213 of the 1st edition. (English translation, pp. 185 and 186.)

[2] Feder, " Ueber Raum und Causalität." sect. 29.

[3] G. E. Schulze, " Kritik der theoretischen Philosophie," vol. ii.
p. 422 *sqq.*

[4] For instance, in Fries' " Kritik der Vernunft," vol. ii. p. 85.

much, that his spirit might truly say to me, in the words
of Homer :

Ἀχλὺν δ' αὖ τοι ἀπ' ὀφθαλμῶν ἕλον, ἢ πρὶν ἐπῆεν.[1]

§ 24. *Of the Misapplication of the Law of Causality.*

From the foregoing exposition it follows, that the application of the causal law to anything but *changes* in the
material, empirically given world, is an abuse of it.   For
instance, it is a misapplication to make use of it with reference to physical forces, without which no changes could
take place; or to Matter, *on* which they take place; or to
the world, to which we must in that case attribute an
absolutely objective existence independently of our intellect; indeed in many other cases besides.   I refer the
reader to what I have said on this subject in my chief
work.[2]   Such misapplications always arise, partly, through
our taking the conception of cause, like many other metaphysical and ethical conceptions, in far *too wide* a sense;
partly, through our forgetting that the causal law is certainly a presupposition which we bring with us into the
world, by which the perception of things outside us becomes
possible; but that, just on that account, we are not
authorized in extending beyond the range and independently of our cognitive faculty a principle, which has its
origin in the equipment of that faculty, nor in assuming it
to hold good as the everlasting order of the universe and
of all that exists.

[1] I lifted from thine eyes the darkness which covered them before.
(Tr.'s Ad.)
[2] " Die Welt a. W. u. V." 2nd edition, vol. ii. ch. iv. p. 42 *et seqq.*;
3rd edition, vol. ii. p. 46 *et seqq.*

§ 25. *The Time in which a Change takes place.*

As the Principle of Sufficient Reason of Becoming is
exclusively applicable to *changes*, we must not omit to
mention here, that the ancient philosophers had already
raised the question as to the time in which a change takes
place, there being no possibility of it taking place during
the existence of the preceding state nor after the new
one has supervened. Yet, if we assign a special time to it
between both states, a body would, during this time, be
neither in the first nor in the second state : a dying man,
for instance, would be neither alive nor dead; a body
neither at rest nor in movement : which would be absurd.
The scruples and sophistic subtleties which this question
has evoked, may be found collected together in Sextus
Empiricus " Adv. Mathem." lib. ix. 267-271, and "Hypat."
iii. c. 14 ; the subject is likewise dealt with by Gellius, l.
vi. c. 13—Plato [1] had disposed somewhat cavalierly of this
knotty point, by maintaining that changes take place
suddenly and occupy *no time at all;* they occur, he says,
in the ἐξαίφνης (*in repentino*), which he calls an ἄτοπος
φύσις, ἐν χρόνῳ οὐδὲν οὖσα ; a strange, timeless existence
(which nevertheless comes within Time).

It was accordingly reserved for the perspicacity of Aristotle to clear up this difficult point, which he has done
profoundly and exhaustively in the sixth Book of Physics,
chap. i.-viii. His proof that no change takes place suddenly (in Plato's ἐξαίφνης), but that each occurs only
gradually and therefore occupies a certain time, is based
entirely upon the pure, *à priori* intuition of Time and of
Space; but it is also very subtle. The pith of this very
lengthy demonstration may, however, be reduced to the
following propositions. When we say of objects that they

---

[1] Plato, " Parmenides," p. 138, ed. B:p.

limit each other, we mean, that both have their extreme
ends in common; therefore only two extended things can
be conterminous, never two indivisible ones, for then they
would be *one*—*i.e.* only lines, but not mere points, can be
conterminous. He then transfers this from Space to Time.
As there always remains a line between two points, so there
always remains a time between two *nows;* this is the time
in which a change takes place—*i.e.* when *one* state is in the
first, and *another* in the second, *now.* This time, like every
other, is divisible to infinity; consequently, whatever is
changing passes through an infinite number of degrees
within that time, through which the second state gradually
grows out of that *first* one.—The process may perhaps be
made more intelligible by the following explanation. Between two consecutive states the difference of which is
perceptible to our senses, there are always several intermediate states, the difference between which is not perceptible to us; because, in order to be sensuously perceptible, the newly arising state must have reached a
certain degree of intensity or of magnitude: it is therefore
preceded by degrees of lesser intensity or extension, in
passing through which it gradually arises. Taken collec-
tively, these are comprised under the name of *change,*
and the time occupied by them is called *the time of change.*
Now, if we apply this to a body being propelled, the first
effect is a certain vibration of its inner parts, which, after
communicating the impulse to other parts, breaks out into
external motion.—Aristotle infers quite rightly from the
infinite divisibility of Time, that everything which fills it,
therefore every change, *i.e.* every passage from one state to
another, must likewise be susceptible of endless subdivision,
so that all that arises, does so in fact by the concourse of
an infinite multitude of parts; accordingly its genesis is
always gradual, never sudden. From these principles and
the consequent gradual arising of each movement, he

draws the weighty inference in the last chapter of this Book, that nothing indivisible, no mere *point* can move. And with this conclusion Kant's definition of Matter, as "that which moves in Space," completely harmonizes.

This law of the continuity and gradual taking place of all changes which Aristotle was thus the first to lay down and prove, we find stated three times by Kant: in his "Dissertatio de mundi sensibilis et intelligibilis forma," § 14, in the "Critique of Pure Reason," [1] and finally in his "Metaphysical First Principles of Natural Science." [2] In all three places his exposition is brief, but also less thorough than that of Aristotle; still, in the main, both entirely agree. We can therefore hardly doubt that, directly or indirectly, Kant must have derived these ideas from Aristotle, though he does not mention him. Aristotle's proposition—οὐκ ἔστι ἀλλήλων ἐχόμενα τὰ νῦν ("the moments of the present are not continuous")—we here find expressed as follows: "between two moments there is always a time," to which may be objected that "even between two centuries there is none; because in Time as in Space, there must always be a pure limit."—Thus Kant, instead of mentioning Aristotle, endeavours in the first and earliest of his three statements to identify the theory he is advancing with Leibnitz' *lex continuitatis*. If they really were the same, Leibnitz must have derived his from Aristotle. Now Leibnitz [3] first stated this *Loi de la continuité* in a letter to Bayle.[4] There, however, he calls it *Principe de l'ordre général*, and gives under this name a very general, vague, chiefly geometrical argumentation, having no direct bearing on the time of change, which he does not even mention.

---

[1] Kant, "Krit. d. r. Vern." 1st edition, p. 207; 5th edition, p. 253. (English translation by M. Müller, p. 182.)

[2] Kant, "Metaphysische Anfangsgründe der Naturwissenschaft." End of the "Allgemeine Anmerkung zur Mechanik."

[3] According to his own assertion, p. 189 of the "Opera philos." ed. Erdmann.   [4] *Ibid.* p. 104.

CHAPTER V.

§ 26. *Explanation of this Class of Objects.*

THE only essential distinction between the human race
and animals, which from time immemorial has been
attributed to a special cognitive faculty peculiar to mankind, called *Reason*, is based upon the fact that man owns
a class of representations which is not shared by any
animal. These are *conceptions*, therefore *abstract*, as opposed
to *intuitive*, representations, from which they are nevertheless derived. The immediate consequence of this is, that
animals can neither speak nor laugh; but indirectly all
those various, important characteristics which distinguish
human from animal life are its consequence. For, through
the supervention of abstract representation, motivation has
now changed its character. Although human actions result
with a necessity no less rigorous than that which rules the
actions of animals, yet through this new kind of motivation—so far as here it consists in *thoughts* which render
elective decision (*i.e.* a conscious conflict of motives) possible—action with a purpose, with reflection, according to
plans and principles, in concert with others, &c. &c., now
takes the place of mere impulse given by present, perceptible
objects; but by this it gives rise to all that renders human
life so rich, so artificial, and so terrible, that man, in this

Western Hemisphere, where his skin has become bleached, and where the primitive, true, profound religions of his first home could not follow him, now no longer recognises animals as his brethren, and falsely believes them to differ fundamentally from him, seeking to confirm this illusion by calling them brutes, giving degrading names to the vital functions which they have in common with him, and proclaiming them outlaws; and thus he hardens his heart against that identity of being between them and himself, which is nevertheless constantly obtruding itself upon him.

Still, as we have said, the whole difference lies in this—that, besides the intuitive representations examined in the last chapter, which are shared by animals, other, abstract representations derived from these intuitive ones, are lodged in the human brain, which is chiefly on this account so much larger than that of animals. Representations of this sort have been called *conceptions*,[1] because each comprehends innumerable individual things in, or rather under, itself, and thus forms a complex.[2] We may also define them as *representations drawn from representations*. For, in forming them, the faculty of abstraction decomposes the complete, intuitive representations described in our last chapter into their component parts, in order to think each of these parts separately as the different qualities of, or relations between, things. By this process, however, the representations necessarily forfeit their perceptibility; just as water, when decomposed, ceases to be fluid and visible. For although each quality thus isolated (abstracted) can quite well be *thought* by itself, it does not at all follow that it can be *perceived* by itself. We form conceptions by dropping a good deal of what is given us in perception, in order to be

[1] *Begriff*, comprehensive thought, derived from *begreifen*, to comprehend. [Tr.]

[2] *Inbegriff*, comprehensive totality. [Tr.]

able to think the rest by itself. To conceive therefore, is to think less than we perceive. If, after considering divers objects of perception, we drop something different belonging to each, yet retain what is the same in all, the result will be the *genus* of that species. The generic conception is accordingly always the conception of every species comprised under it, after deducting all that does not belong to *every* species. Now, as every possible conception may be thought as a *genus*, a conception is always something general, and as such, not perceptible. Every conception has on this account also its *sphere*, as the sum-total [1] of what may be thought under it. The higher we ascend in abstract thought, the more we deduct, the less therefore remains to be thought. The highest, *i.e.* the most general conceptions, are the emptiest and poorest, and at last become mere husks, such as, for instance, being, essence, thing, becoming, &c. &c.—Of what avail, by the way, can philosophical systems be, which are only spun out of conceptions of this sort and have for their substance mere flimsy husks of thoughts like these? They must of necessity be exceedingly empty, poor, and therefore also dreadfully tiresome.

Now as representations, thus sublimated and analysed to form abstract conceptions, have, as we have said, forfeited all perceptibility, they would entirely escape our consciousness, and be of no avail to it for the thinking processes to which they are destined, were they not fixed and retained in our senses by arbitrary signs. These signs are words. In as far as they constitute the contents of dictionaries and therefore of language, words always designate *general* representations, conceptions, never perceptible objects; whereas a lexicon which enumerates individual things, only contains proper names, not words, and is either a geo-

---

[1] *Inbegriff.*

graphical or historical dictionary : that is to say, it enumerates what is separated either by Time or by Space ; for,
as *my* readers know, Time and Space are the *principium
individuationis.* It is only because animals are limited to
intuitive representations and incapable of any abstraction—
incapable therefore of forming conceptions—that they are
without language, even when they are able to articulate
words ; whereas they understand proper names. That it
is this same defect which excludes them from laughter, I
have shown in my theory of the ridiculous.[1]

On analyzing a long, continuous speech made by a man
of no education, we find in it an abundance of logical forms,
clauses, turns of phrase, distinctions, and subtleties of all
sorts, correctly expressed by means of grammatical forms
with their inflections and constructions, and even with a
frequent use of the *sermo obliquus,* of the different moods,
&c. &c., all in conformity with rule, which astonishes us,
and in which we are forced to recognise an extensive and
perfectly coherent knowledge. Still this knowledge has been
acquired on the basis of the perceptible world, the reduction
of whose whole essence to abstract conceptions is the fundamental business of the Reason, and can only take place by
means of language. In learning the use of language therefore, the whole mechanism of Reason—that is, all that
is essential in Logic—is brought to our consciousness. Now
this can evidently not take place without considerable
mental effort and fixed attention, for which the desire to
learn gives children the requisite strength. So long as
that desire has before it what is really available and necessary, it is vigorous, and it only appears weak when we try
to force upon children that which is not suited to their
comprehension. Thus even a coarsely educated child, in
learning all the turns and subtleties of language, as well

---

[1] See "Die Welt a. W. u. V." vol. i. sect. 13, and vol. ii. ch. 8.

through its own conversation as that of others, accomplishes
the development of its Reason, and acquires that really
concrete Logic, which consists less in logical rules than in
the proper application of them ; just as the rules of
harmony are learnt by persons of musical talent simply by
playing the piano, without reading music or studying
thorough-bass.—The deaf and dumb alone are excluded
from the above-mentioned logical training through the
acquirement of speech ; therefore they are almost as un-
reasonable as animals, when they have not been taught to
read by the very artificial means specially adapted for their
requirements, which takes the place of the natural schooling
of Reason.

§ 27. *The Utility of Conceptions.*

The fundamental essence of our Reason or thinking
faculty is, as we have seen, the power of abstraction, or the
faculty of forming *conceptions :* it is therefore the presence
of these in our consciousness which produces such amazing
results.   That it should be able to do this, rests mainly on
the following grounds.

It is just because they contain less than the representations from which they are drawn, that conceptions are
easier to deal with than representations ; they are, in fact,
to these almost as the formula of higher arithmetic to the
mental operations which give rise to them and which they
represent, or as a logarithm to its number.   They only
contain just the part required of the many representations
from which they are drawn ; if instead we were to try
to recall those representations themselves by means of
the imagination, we should, as it were, have to lug about
a load of unessential lumber, which would only embarrass
us ; whereas, by the help of conceptions, we are enabled
to think only those parts and relations of all these repre-

sentations which are wanted for each individual purpose: so that their employment may be compared to doing away with superfluous luggage, or to working with extracts instead of plants themselves—with quinine, instead of bark. What is properly called *thinking*, in its narrowest sense, is the occupation of the intellect with conceptions: that is, the presence in our consciousness of the class of representations we now have before us. This is also what we call *reflection*: a word which, by a figure of speech borrowed from Optics, expresses at once the derivative and the secondary character of this kind of knowledge. Now it is this thinking, this reflection, which gives man that *delibera-tion*, which is wanting in animals. For, by enabling him to think many things under one conception, but always only the essential part in each of them, it allows him to drop at his pleasure every kind of distinction, consequently even those of Time and of Space, and thus he acquires the power of embracing in thought, not only the past and the future, but also what is absent; while animals are in every respect strictly bound to the present. This delibera-tive faculty again is really the root of all those theoretical and practical achievements which give man so great a superiority over animals; first and foremost, of his care for the future while taking the past into consideration; then of his premeditated, systematic, methodical procedure in all undertakings, and therefore of the co-operation of many persons towards a common end, and, by this, of law, order, the State, &c. &c.—But it is especially in Science that the use of conceptions is important; for they are, pro-perly speaking, its materials. The aims of all the sciences may, indeed, in the last resort, be reduced to knowledge of the particular through the general; now this is only possible by means of the *dictum de omni et nullo*, and this, again, is only possible through the existence of conceptions. Aristotle therefore says: ἄνευ μὲν γὰρ τῶν καθόλου οὐκ ἔστιν ἐπιστήμην λαβεῖν [1] (*absque universalibus enim non datur scientia*). Conceptions are precisely those *universalia*, whose mode of existence formed the argument of the long controversy between the Realists and Nominalists in the Middle Ages.

§ 28. *Representatives of Conceptions. The Faculty of Judgment.*

Conceptions must not be confounded with pictures of the imagination, these being intuitive and complete, therefore individual representations, although they are not called forth by sensuous impressions and do not therefore belong to the complex of experience. Even when used to *represent a conception,* a picture of the imagination (phantasm) ought to be distinguished from a conception. We use phantasms as *representatives of conceptions* when we try to grasp the intuitive representation itself that has given rise to the conception and to make it tally with that conception, which is in all cases impossible; for there is no representation, for instance, of dog in general, colour in general, triangle in general, number in general, nor is there any picture of the imagination which corresponds to these conceptions. Then we evoke the phantasm of some dog or other, which, as a representation, must in all cases be determined : that is, it must have a certain size, shape, colour, &c. &c. ; even though the conception represented by it has no such determinations. When we use such *representatives of conceptions* however, we are always conscious that they are not adequate to the conceptions they represent, and that they are full of arbitrary determinations. Towards the end of the first part of his

---

[1] Aristot. "Metaph." xii. c. 9, "For without universals it is impossible to have knowledge." (Tr.'s Add.)

Twelfth Essay on Human Understanding, Hume expresses himself in agreement with this view, as also Rousseau in his "Discours sur l'Origine de l'Inégalité." [1] Kant's doctrine, on the contrary, is a totally different one. The matter is one which introspection and clear reflection can alone decide. Each of us must therefore examine himself as to whether he is conscious in his own conceptions of a "Monogram of Pure Imagination *à priori;*" whether, for instance, when he thinks dog, he is conscious of something *entre chien et loup;* or whether, as I have here explained it, he is either thinking an abstract conception through his Reason, or representing some representative of that conception as a complete picture through his imagination.

All thinking, in a wider sense: that is, all inner activity of the mind in general, necessitates either words or pictures of the imagination: without one or other of these it has nothing to hold by. They are not, however, both necessary at the same time, although they may co-operate to their mutual support. Now, thinking in a narrower sense— that is, abstract reflection by means of words—is either purely logical reasoning, in which case it keeps strictly to its own sphere; or it touches upon the limits of perceptible representations in order to come to an understanding with them, so as to bring that which is given by experience and grasped by perception into connection with abstract conceptions resulting from clear reflection, and thus to gain complete possession of it. In thinking therefore, we seek either for the conception or rule to which a given perception belongs, or for the particular case which proves a given conception or rule. In this quality, thinking is an activity of the *faculty of judgment,* and indeed in the first case a reflective, in the second, a subsuming activity. The faculty of judgment is accordingly the mediator between intuitive and abstract knowledge, or between the Under-

---

[1] Part the First, in the middle.

derstanding and the Reason. In most men it has merely rudimentary, often even merely nominal existence;[1] they are destined to follow the lead of others, and it is as well not to converse with them more than is necessary.

The true kernel of all knowledge is that reflection which works with the help of intuitive representations; for it goes back to the fountain-head, to the basis of all conceptions. Therefore it generates all really original thoughts, all primary and fundamental views and all inventions, so far as chance had not the largest share in them. *The Understanding* prevails in this sort of thinking, whilst *the Reason* is the chief factor in purely abstract reflection. Certain thoughts which wander about for a long time in our heads, belong to this sort of reflection : thoughts which come and go, now clothed in one kind of intuition, now in another, until they at last become clear, fix themselves in conceptions and find words to express them. Some, indeed, never find words to express them, and these are, unfortunately, the best of all: *quæ voce meliora sunt,* as Apuleius says.

Aristotle, however, went too far in thinking that no reflection is possible without pictures of the imagination. Nevertheless, what he says on this point,[2] οὐδέποτε νοεῖ ἄνευ φαντάσματος ἡ ψυχή (*anima sine phantasmate nunquam intelligit*),[3] and ὅταν θεωρῇ, ἀνάγκη ἅμα φάντασμά τι θεωρεῖν (*qui contemplatur, necesse est, una cum phantasmate contempletur*),[4] and again, νοεῖν οὐκ ἔστι ἄνευ φαντάσματος (*fieri non potest, ut sine phantasmate quidquam intelli-*

---

[1] Let any one to whom this assertion may appear hyperbolical, consider the fate of Göthe's " Theory of Colours" (*Farbenlehre*), and should he wonder at my finding a corroboration for it in that fate, he will himself have corroborated it a second time.

[2] Aristot. " De anima," iii. c. c. 3, 7, 8.

[3] " The mind never thinks without (the aid of) an image." [Tr.]

[4] " He who observes anything must observe some image along with it." [Tr.]

gatur),[1]—made a strong impression upon the thinkers of the fifteenth and sixteenth centuries, who therefore frequently and emphatically repeat what he says. Pico della Mirandola,[2] for instance, says: *Necesse est, eum, qui ratiocinatur et intelligit, phantasmata speculari;*—Melanchthon[3] says: *Oportet intelligentem phantasmata speculari;*—and Jord. Brunus[4] says, *dicit Aristoteles: oportet scire volentem, phantasmata speculari.* Pomponatius[5] expresses himself in the same sense.—On the whole, all that can be affirmed is, that every true and primary notion, every genuine philosophic theorem even, must have some sort of intuitive view for its innermost kernel or root. This, though something momentary[6] and single, subsequently imparts life and spirit to the whole analysis, however exhaustive it may be,—just as one drop of the right reagent suffices to tinge a whole solution with the colour of the precipitate which it causes. When an analysis has a kernel of this sort, it is like a bank note issued by a firm which has ready money wherewith to back it; whereas every other analysis proceeding from mere combinations of abstract conceptions, resembles a bank note which is issued by a firm which has nothing but other paper obligations to back it with. All mere rational talk thus renders the result of given conceptions clearer, but does not, strictly speaking, bring anything new to light. It might therefore be left to each individual to do himself, instead of filling whole volumes every day.

§ 29. *Principle of Sufficient Reason of Knowing.*

But, even in a narrower sense, thinking does not consist in the bare presence of abstract conceptions in our con-

---

[1] " De Memoria," c. 1 : " It is impossible to think without (the aid of) an image."   [2] " De imaginatione," c. 5.

[3] " De anima," p. 130.   [4] " De compositione imaginum," p. 10.

[5] " De immortalitate," pp. 54 et 70.

[6] " *Ein Momentanes und Einheitliches.*"

sciousness, but rather in connecting or separating two or more of these conceptions under sundry restrictions and modifications which Logic indicates in the Theory of Judgments. A relation of this sort between conceptions distinctly thought and expressed we call a *judgment*. Now, with reference to these judgments, the Principle of Sufficient Reason here once more holds good, yet in a widely different form from that which has been explained in the preceding chapter; for here it appears as the Principle of Sufficient Reason of Knowing, *principium rationis sufficientis cognoscendi*. As such, it asserts that if a *judgment* is to express *knowledge* of any kind, it must have a sufficient reason : in virtue of which quality it then receives the predicate *true*. Thus *truth* is the reference of a judgment to something different from itself, called its reason or ground, which reason, as we shall presently see, itself admits of a considerable variety of kinds. As, however, this reason is invariably a something upon which the judgment rests, the German term for it, viz., *Grund*, is not ill chosen. In Latin, and in all languages of Latin origin, the word by which a reason of knowledge is designated, is the same as that used for the faculty of Reason (*ratiocinatio*) : both are called *ratio, la ragione, la razon, la raison, the reason*. From this it is evident, that attaining knowledge of the reasons of judgments had been recognised as Reason's highest function, its business κατ᾽ ἐξοχήν. Now, these grounds upon which a judgment may rest, may be divided into *four* different kinds, and the truth obtained by that judgment will correspondingly differ. They are stated in the following paragraph.

§ 30. *Logical Truth.*

A judgment may have for its reason another judgment; in this case it has *logical* or *formal* truth. Whether it has

material truth also, remains an open question and depends
on whether the judgment on which it rests has material
truth, or whether the series of judgments on which it is
founded leads to a judgment which has material truth, or
not. This founding of a judgment upon another judgment
always originates in a comparison between them which
takes place either directly, by mere conversion or contra-
position, or by adding a third judgment, and then the truth
of the judgment we are founding becomes evident through
their mutual relation. This operation is the complete
syllogism. It is brought about either by the opposition or
by the subsumption of conceptions. As the syllogism,
which is the founding of one judgment upon another by
means of a third, never has to do with anything but judgments; and as judgments are only combinations of conceptions, and conceptions again are the exclusive object of our
Reason : syllogizing has been rightly called Reason's special
function. The whole syllogistic science, in fact, is nothing
but the sum-total of the rules for applying the principle of
sufficient reason to the mutual relations of judgments ;
consequently it is the canon of *logical truth*.

Judgments, whose truth becomes evident through the
four well-known laws of thinking, must likewise be regarded
as based upon other judgments ; for these four laws are
themselves precisely judgments, from which follows the
truth of those other judgments. For instance, the judgment : " A triangle is a space enclosed within three lines,"
has for its last reason the Principle of Identity, that is to
say, the thought expressed by that principle. The judgment, " No body is without extension," has for its last
reason the Principle of Contradiction. This again, " Every
judgment is either true or untrue," has for its last reason
the Principle of the Excluded Middle ; and finally, " No
one can admit anything to be true without knowing
why," has for its last reason the Principle of Sufficient

Reason of Knowing. In the general employment of our Reason, we do not, it is true, before admitting them to be true, reduce judgments which follow from the four laws of thinking to their last reasons, as premisses; for most men are even ignorant of the very existence of these abstract laws. The dependence of such judgments upon them, as their premisses, is however no more diminished by this, than the dependence of the first judgment upon the second, as its premiss, is diminished by the fact, that it is not at all necessary for the principle, " all bodies incline towards the centre of the earth," to be present in the consciousness of any one who says, " this body will fall if its support is removed." That in Logic, therefore, *intrinsic truth* should hitherto have been attributed to all judgments founded exclusively on the four laws of thinking: that is to say, that these judgments should have been pronounced *directly true*, and that this *intrinsic logical truth* should have been distinguished from *extrinsic logical truth*, as attributed to all judgments which have another judgment for their reason, I cannot approve. Every truth is the reference of a judgment to something *outside* of it, and the term *intrinsic truth* is a contradiction.

§ 31. *Empirical Truth.*

A judgment may be founded upon a representation of the first class, *i.e.* a perception by means of the senses, consequently on experience. In this case it has *material truth*, and moreover, if the judgment is founded *immediately* on experience, this truth is *empirical truth*.

When we say, " A judgment has *material truth*," we mean on the whole, that its conceptions are connected, separated, limited, according to the requirements of the intuitive representations through which it is inferred. To attain knowledge of this, is the direct function of the *faculty of judgment,* as the mediator between the intuitive and the abstract or discursive faculty of knowing—in other words, between the Understanding and the Reason.

§ 32. *Transcendental Truth.*

The *forms* of intuitive, empirical knowledge which lie within the Understanding and pure Sensibility may, as conditions of all possible experience, be the grounds of a judgment, which is in that case synthetical *à priori.* As nevertheless this kind of judgment has material truth, its truth is *transcendental;* because the judgment is based not only on experience, but on the conditions of all possible experience lying within us. For it is determined precisely by that which determines experience itself: namely, either by the forms of Space and of Time perceived by us *à priori,* or by the causal law, known to us *à priori.* Propositions such as : two straight lines do not include a space; nothing happens without a cause; matter can neither come into being nor perish ; $3 \times 7 = 21$, are examples of this kind of judgment. The whole of pure Mathematics, and no less my tables of the *Prædicabilia à priori,*[1] as well as most of Kant's theorems in his " Metaphysische Anfangsgründe der Naturwissenschaft," may, properly speaking, be adduced in corroboration of this kind of truth.

§. 33. *Metalogical Truth.*

Lastly, a judgment may be founded on the formal conditions of all thinking, which are contained in the Reason ; and in this case its truth is of a kind which seems to me best defined as *metalogical truth.* This expression has nothing at all to do with the " Metalogicus " written by Johannes

---

[1] See " Die Welt a. W. u. V." 3rd edition, vol. ii. ch. iv. p. 55.

Sarisberriensis in the twelfth century, for he declares in his prologue, " *quia Logicæ suscepi patrocinium, Metalogicus inscriptus est liber,*" and never makes use of the word again. There are only four metalogically true judgments of this sort, which were discovered long ago by induction, and called the laws of all thinking; although entire uniformity of opinion as to their expression and even as to their number has not yet been arrived at, whereas all agree perfectly as to what they are on the whole meant to indicate. They are the following :—

1. A subject is equal to the sum total of its predicates, or a = a.

2. No predicate can be attributed and denied to a subject at the same time, or a = — a = o.

3. One of two opposite, contradictory predicates must belong to every subject.

4. Truth is the reference of a judgment to something outside of it, as its sufficient reason.

It is by means of a kind of reflection which I am inclined to call Reason's self-examination, that we know that these judgments express the conditions of all thinking, and therefore have these conditions for their reason. For, by the fruitlessness of its endeavours to think in opposition to these laws, our Reason acknowledges them to be the conditions of all possible thinking: we then find out, that it is just as impossible to think in opposition to them, as it is to move the members of our body in a contrary direction to their joints. If it were possible for the subject to know itself, these laws would be known to us *immediately*, and we should not need to try experiments with them on objects, *i.e.* representations. In this respect it is just the same with the reasons of judgments which have transcendental truth; for they do not either come into our consciousness immediately, but only in *concreto*, by means of objects, *i.e.* of representations. In endeavouring, for instance, to conceive a change without a preceding cause, or a passing into or out of being of Matter, we become aware that it is impossible; moreover we recognise this impossibility to be an objective one, although its root lies in our intellect: for we could not otherwise bring it to consciousness in a subjective way. There is, on the whole, a strong likeness and connection between transcendental and metalogical truths, which shows that they spring from a common root. In this chapter we see the Principle of Sufficient Reason chiefly as metalogical truth, whereas in the last it appeared as transcendental truth and in the next one it will again be seen as transcendental truth under another form. In the present treatise I am taking special pains, precisely on this account, to establish the Principle of Sufficient Reason as a judgment having a fourfold reason; by which I do not mean four different reasons leading contingently to the same judgment, but one reason presenting itself under a fourfold aspect: and this is what I call its Fourfold Root. The other three metalogical truths so strongly resemble one another, that in considering them one is almost necessarily induced to search for their common expression, as I have done in the Ninth Chapter of the Second Volume of my chief work. On the other hand, they differ considerably from the Principle of Sufficient Reason. If we were to seek an analogue for the three other metalogical truths among transcendental truths, the one I should choose would be this: Substance, I mean Matter, is permanent.

§ 34. *Reason.*

As the class of representations I have dealt with in this chapter belongs exclusively to Man, and as all that distinguishes human life so forcibly from that of animals

and confers so great a superiority on man, is, as we have
shown, based upon his faculty for these representations,
this faculty evidently and unquestionably constitutes that
Reason, which from time immemorial has been reputed
the prerogative of mankind. Likewise all that has been
considered by all nations and in all times explicitly as
the work or manifestation of the Reason, of the λόγος,
λόγιμον, λογιστικόν, *ratio, la ragione, la razon, la raison,
reason,* may evidently also be reduced to what is only
possible for abstract, discursive, reflective, mediate knowledge, conditioned by words, and not for mere intuitive,
immediate, sensuous knowledge, which belongs to animals
also.   Cicero rightly places *ratio et oratio* together,[1] and de-
scribes them as *quæ docendo, discendo, communicando, discep-
tando, judicando, conciliat inter se homines,* &c. &c., and [2]
*rationem dico, et, si placet, pluribus verbis, mentem, consilium,
cogitationem, prudentiam.* And [3] *ratio, qua una præstamus
beluis, per quam conjectura valemus, argumentamur, refelli-
mus, disserimus, conficimus aliquid, concludimus.* But, in all
ages and countries, philosophers have invariably expressed
themselves in this sense with respect to the Reason, even to
Kant himself, who still defines it as the faculty for principles and for inference; although it cannot be denied that
he first gave rise to the distorted views which followed. In
my principal work,[4] and also in the Fundamental Problems of Ethics, I have spoken at great length about the
agreement of all philosophers on this point, as well as
about the true nature of Reason, as opposed to the distorted conceptions for which we have to thank the pro-

[1] Cicer. " De Offic." i. 16.   *Idem,* " De nat. deor." ii. 7.
[3] *Idem,* " De Leg." i. 10.
[4] See "Die Welt a. W. u. V." 2nd edition, vol. i. § 8, and also in
the Appendix, pp. 577-585 (3rd edition, pp. 610-620), and again vol. ii.
ch. vi. ; finally " Die b. G-P. d. Ethik," pp. 148-154 (2nd edition,
pp. 146-151).

fessors of philosophy of this century. I need not therefore repeat what has already been said there, and shall limit myself to the following considerations.

Our professors of philosophy have thought fit to do away with the name which had hitherto been given to that faculty of thinking and pondering by means of reflection and conceptions, which distinguishes man from animals, which necessitates language while it qualifies us for its use, with which all human deliberation and all human achievements hang together, and which had therefore always been viewed in this light and understood in this sense by all nations and even by all philosophers. In defiance of all sound taste and custom, our professors decided that this faculty should henceforth be called *Understanding* instead of *Reason*, and that all that is derived from it should be named *intelligent* instead of *rational*, which, of course, had a strange, awkward ring about it, like a discordant tone in music. For in all ages and countries the words *understanding*, *intellectus, acumen, perspicacia, sagacitas*, &c. &c., had been used to denote the more intuitive faculty described in our last chapter; and its results, which differ specifically from those of Reason here in question, have always been called *intelligent, sagacious, clever*, &c. &c. *Intelligent* and *rational* were accordingly always distinguished one from the other, as manifestations of two entirely and widely different mental faculties. Our professional philosophers could not, however, take this into account; their policy required the sacrifice, and in such cases the cry is : " Move on, truth ; for we have higher, well-defined aims in view ! Make way for us, truth, *in majorem Dei gloriam*, as thou hast long ago learnt to do ! Is it thou who givest fees and pensions ? Move on, truth, move on ; betake thyself to merit and crouch in the corner ! " The fact was, they wanted Reason's place and name for a faculty of their own creation and fabrication, or to speak more correctly and honestly, for a

completely fictitious faculty, destined to help them out of
the straits to which Kant had reduced them ; a faculty
for direct, metaphysical knowledge : that is to say, one
which transcends all possible experience, is able to grasp
the world of things in themselves and their relations, and
is therefore, before all, consciousness of God (*Gottesbewusst-*
sein) : that is, it knows God the Lord immediately, con-
strues *à priori* the way in which he has created the Universe,
or, should this sound too trivial, the way in which he has produced it out of himself, or to a certain degree generated it
by some more or less necessary vital process, or again—as
the most convenient proceeding, however comical it may
appear—simply " dismissed " it, according to the custom
of sovereigns at the end of an audience, and left it to get
upon its legs by itself and walk away wherever it liked.
Nothing less than the impudence of a scribbler of nonsense
like Hegel, could, it is true, be found to venture upon this
last step. Yet it is tom-foolery like this which, largely
amplified, has filled hundreds of volumes for the last fifty
years under the name of cognitions of Reason (*Vernunfter-*
kenntnisse), and forms the argument of so many works
called philosophical by their authors, and scientific by others
—one would think ironically—this expression being even
repeated to satiety. *Reason*, to which all this wisdom
is falsely and audaciously imputed, is pronounced to be
a " supersensuous faculty," or a faculty "for ideas ;"
in short, an oracular power lying within us, designed
directly for Metaphysics. During the last half-century,
however, there has been considerable discrepancy of opinion
among the adepts as to the way in which all these supersensuous wonders are perceived. According to the most
audacious, Reason has a direct intuition of the Absolute,
or even *ad libitum* of the Infinite and of its evolutions towards the Finite. Others, somewhat less bold, opine that
its mode of receiving this information partakes rather of

audition than of vision ; since it does not exactly see, but merely *hears* (*vernimmt*), what is going on in " cloud-cuckoo-land " (νεφελοκοκκυγία), and then honestly transmits what it has thus received to the Understanding, to be worked up into text-books. According to a pun of Jacobi's, even the German name for Reason, " *Vernunft*," is derived from this pretended " *Vernehmen ;* " whereas it evidently comes from that " *Vernehmen* " which is conveyed by language and conditioned by Reason, and by which the distinct perception of words and their meaning is designated, as opposed to mere sensuous hearing which animals have also. This miserable *jeu de mots* nevertheless continues, after half a century, to find favour; it passes for a serious thought, nay even for a proof, and has been repeated over and over again. The most modest among the adepts again assert, that Reason neither sees nor hears, therefore it receives neither a vision nor a report of all these wonders, and has a mere vague *Ahndung*, or misgiving of them ; but then they drop the *d*, by which the word (*Ahnung*) acquires a peculiar touch of silliness, which, backed up as it is by the sheepish look of the apostle for the time being of this wisdom, cannot fail to gain it entrance.

My readers know that I only admit the word *idea* in its primitive, that is Platonic, sense, and that I have treated this point at length and exhaustively in the Third Book of my chief work. The French and English, on the other hand, certainly attach a very commonplace, but quite clear and definite meaning to the word *idée*, or *idea ;* whereas the Germans lose their heads as soon as they hear the word *Ideen;* [1] all presence of mind abandons them, and they feel as if they were about to ascend in a balloon. Here therefore was a field of action for our adepts in intellectual intuition ; so the most impudent of them, the notorious *charlatan*

---

[1] Here Schopenhauer adds, "especially when pronounced *Uedähen*." [Tr.]

Hegel, without more ado, called his theory of the universe and of all things "*Die Idee*," and in this of course all thought that they had something to lay hold of. Still, if we inquire into the nature of these *ideas* for which Reason is pronounced to be the faculty, without letting ourselves be put out of countenance, the explanation usually given is an empty, high-flown, confused verbiage, in set periods of such length, that if the reader does not fall asleep before he has half read it, he will find himself bewildered rather than enlightened at the end; nay, he may even have a suspicion that these ideas are very like chimæras. Meanwhile, should anyone show a desire to know more about this sort of ideas, he will have all kinds of things served up to him. Now it will be the chief subjects of the theses of Scholasticism— I allude here to the representations of God, of an immortal Soul, of a real, objectively existent World and its laws— which Kant himself has unfortunately called Ideas of Reason, erroneously and unjustifiably, as I have shown in my Critique of his philosophy, yet merely with a view to proving the utter impossibility of demonstrating them and their want of all theoretical authority. Then again it will be, as a variation, only God, Freedom, and Immortality; at other times it will be the Absolute, whose acquaintance we have already made in § 20, as the Cosmological Proof, forced to travel incognito; or the Infinite as opposed to the Finite; for, on the whole, the German reader is disposed to content himself with such empty talk as this, without perceiving that the only clear thought he can get out of it is, 'that which has an end' and 'that which has none.' 'The Good, the True, and the Beautiful,' moreover, stand high in favour with the sentimental and tender-hearted as pretended *ideas*, though they are really only three very wide and abstract conceptions, because they are extracted from a multitude of things and relations; wherefore, like many other such *abstracta*, they are exceedingly empty. As regards their contents, I have shown above (§ 29) that Truth is a quality belonging exclusively to judgments: that is, a logical quality; and as to the other two *abstracta*, I refer my readers partly to § 65 of the first volume, partly to the entire Third Book of my chief work. If, nevertheless, a very solemn and mysterious air is assumed and the eyebrows are raised up to the wig whenever these three meagre *abstracta* are mentioned, young people may easily be induced to believe that something peculiar and inexpressible lies behind them, which entitles them to be called *ideas*, and harnessed to the triumphal car of this would-be metaphysical Reason.

When therefore we are told, that we possess a faculty for direct, material (*i.e.*, not only formal, but substantial), supersensuous knowledge, (that is, a knowledge which transcends all possible experience), a faculty specially designed for metaphysical insight, and inherent in us for this purpose—I must take the liberty to call this a downright lie. For the slightest candid self-examination will suffice to convince us that absolutely no such faculty resides within us. The result at which all honest, competent, authoritative thinkers have arrived in the course of ages, moreover, tallies exactly with my assertion. It is as follows: All that is innate in the whole of our cognitive faculty, all that is therefore *à priori* and independent of experience, is strictly limited to the *formal* part of knowledge: that is, to the consciousness of the peculiar functions of the intellect and of the only way in which they can possibly act; but in order to give material knowledge, these functions one and all require material from outside. Within us therefore lie the forms of external, objective perception: Time and Space, and then the law of Causality—as a mere form of the Understanding which enables it to construct the objective, corporeal world— finally, the formal part of abstract knowledge: this last is deposited and treated of in *Logic*, which our forefathers

therefore rightly called the *Theory of Reason*. But this
very Logic teaches us also, that the *conceptions* which constitute those judgments and conclusions to which all logical
laws refer, must look to *intuitive* knowledge for their *material*
and their *content;* just as the Understanding, which creates
this intuitive knowledge, looks to sensation for the material
which gives content to its *à priori* forms.

Thus all that is *material* in our knowledge : that is to say,
all that cannot be reduced to subjective *form,* to individual
mode of activity, to functions of our intellect,—its whole
material therefore,—comes from outside ; that is, in the last
resort, from the objective perception of the corporeal world,
which has its origin in sensation.   Now it is this intuitive
and, so far as material content is concerned, empirical
knowledge, which *Reason—real* Reason—works up into conceptions, which it fixes sensuously by means of words; these
conceptions then supply the materials for its endless combinations through judgments and conclusions, which constitute
the weft of our thought-world. *Reason* therefore has absolutely no *material,* but merely a *formal,* content, and this is
the object-matter of Logic, which consequently contains only
forms and rules for thinking operations.   In reflecting,
Reason is absolutely forced to take its material contents
from outside, *i.e.,* from the intuitive representations which
the Understanding has created. Its functions are exercised
on them, first of all, in forming *conceptions,* by dropping
some of the various qualities of things while retaining others,
which are then connected together to a conception. Representations, however, forfeit their capacity for being intuitively perceived by this process, while they become easier to
deal with, as has already been shown.   It is therefore in
this, and in this alone, that the efficiency of Reason consists;
whereas it can never supply *material content from its own resources.*—It has nothing but forms : its nature is feminine ;
it only conceives, but does not generate.   It is not by mere

chance that the Reason is feminine in all Latin, as well as Teutonic, languages; whereas the Understanding is invariably masculine.

In using such expressions as 'sound Reason teaches this,' or 'Reason should control passion,' we by no means imply that Reason furnishes material knowledge out of its own resources; but rather do we point to the results of rational reflection, that is, to logical inference from principles which abstract knowledge has gradually gathered from experience and by which we obtain a clear and comprehensive view, not only of what is empirically necessary, and may therefore, the case occurring, be foreseen, but even of the reasons and consequences of our own deeds also. *Reasonable* or *rational* is everywhere synonymous with *consistent* or *logical*, and conversely; for Logic is only Reason's natural procedure itself, expressed in a system of rules; therefore these expressions (rational and logical) stand in the same relation to one another as theory and practice. Exactly in this same sense too, when we speak of a reasonable conduct, we mean by it one which is quite consistent, one therefore which proceeds from general conceptions, and is not determined by the transitory impression of the moment. By this, however, the morality of such conduct is in no wise determined: it may be good or bad indifferently. Detailed explanations of all this are to be found in my " Critique of Kant's Philosophy," [1] and also in my " Fundamental Problems of Ethics." [2] Notions derived from *pure Reason* are, lastly, those which have their source in the *formal* part, whether intuitive or reflective, of our cognitive faculty; those, consequently, which we are able to bring to our consciousness *à priori*, that is, without

[1] " Die Welt a. W. u. V." 2nd edition, vol. i. p. 576 *et seqq.*; 3rd edition, p. 610 *et seq.*

[2] Schopenhauer, "Die beiden Grundprobleme der Ethik," p. 152; 2nd edition, p. 149 *et seq.*

the help of experience. They are invariably based upon principles which have transcendental or metalogical truth.

A Reason, on the other hand, which supplies material knowledge primarily out of its own resources and conveys positive information transcending the sphere of possible experience; a Reason which, in order to do this, must necessarily contain *innate ideas*, is a pure fiction, invented by our professional philosophers and a product of the terror with which Kant's Critique of Pure Reason has inspired them. I wonder now, whether these gentlemen know a certain Locke and whether they have ever read his works? Perhaps they may have done so in times long gone by, cursorily and superficially, while looking down complacently on this great thinker from the heights of their own conscious superiority: may be, too, in some inferior German translation; for I do not yet see that the knowledge of modern languages has increased in proportion to the deplorable decrease in that of ancient ones. How could time besides be found for such old croakers as Locke, when even a real, thorough knowledge of Kant's Philosophy at present hardly exists excepting in a very few, very old heads? The youth of the generation now at its maturity had of course to be spent in the study of "Hegel's gigantic mind," of the "sublime Schleiermacher," and of the "acute Herbart." Alas! alas! the great mischief in academical hero-worship of this sort, and in the glorification of university celebrities by worthy colleagues in office or hopeful aspirants to it, is precisely, that ordinary intellects—Nature's mere manufactured ware—are presented to honest credulous youths of immature judgment, as master minds, exceptions and ornaments of mankind. The students forthwith throw all their energies into the barren study of the endless, insipid scribblings of such mediocrities, thus wasting the short, invaluable period allotted to them for higher education, instead of using it

to attain the sound information they might have found in
the works of those extremely rare, genuine, truly exceptional thinkers, *nantes in gurgite vasto*, who only rise to the
surface every now and then in the course of ages, because
Nature produced but one of each kind, and then "destroyed
the mould." For this generation also those great minds
might have had life, had our youth not been cheated out
of its share in their wisdom by these exceedingly pernicious
extollers of mediocrity, members of the vast league and
brotherhood of mediocrities, which is as flourishing to-day
as it ever was and still hoists its flag as high as it can in
persistent antagonism to all that is great and genuine,
as humiliating to its members. Thanks to them, our age
has declined to so low an ebb, that Kant's Philosophy,
which it took our fathers years of study, of serious application and of strenuous effort to understand, has again
become foreign to the present generation, which stands
before it like ὄνος πρὸς λύραν, at times attacking it coarsely
and clumsily—as barbarians throw stones at the statue of
some Greek god which is foreign to them. Now, as this is
the case, I feel it incumbent upon me to advise all cham-
pions of a Reason that perceives, comprehends, and knows
directly—in short, that supplies material knowledge out of
its own resources—to read, as something new to them, the
First Book of Locke's work, which has been celebrated
throughout the world for the last hundred and fifty years,
and in it especially to peruse §§ 21-26 of the Third Chapter, expressly directed against all innate notions. For
although Locke goes too far in denying all innate truths,
inasmuch as he extends his denial even to our *formal*
knowledge—a point in which he has been brilliantly recti-
fied by Kant—he is nevertheless perfectly and undeniably
right with reference to all *material* knowledge : that is, all
knowledge which gives substance.

I have already said in my Ethics what I must nevertheless repeat here, because, as the Spanish proverb says, *"No huy peor sordo que quien no quiere oir"* (None so deaf as those who will not hear): namely, that if Reason were a faculty specially designed for Metaphysics, a faculty which supplied the material of knowledge and could reveal that which transcends all possible experience, the same harmony would necessarily reign between men on metaphysical and religious subjects—for they are identical—as on mathematical ones, and those who differed in opinion from the rest would simply be looked upon as not quite right in their mind. Now exactly the contrary takes place, for on no subject are men so completely at variance with one another as upon these. Ever since men first began to think, philosophical systems have opposed and combated each other everywhere; they are, in fact, often diametrically contrary to one another. Ever since men first began to believe (which is still longer), religions have fought against one another with fire and sword, with excommunication and cannons. But in times when faith was most ardent, it was not the lunatic asylum, but the Inquisition, with all its paraphernalia, which awaited individual heretics. Here again, therefore, experience flatly and categorically contradicts the false assertion, that Reason is a faculty for direct metaphysical knowledge, or, to speak more clearly, of inspiration from above. Surely it is high time that severe judgment should be passed upon this Reason, since, *horribile dictu*, so lame, so palpable a falsehood continues after half a century to be hawked about all over Germany, wandering year by year from the professors' chair to the students' bench, and from bench to chair, and has actually found a few simpletons, even in France, willing to believe in it, and carry it about in that country also. Here, however, French *bon-sens* will very soon send *la raison transcendentale* about its business.

But where was this falsehood originally hatched? How did the fiction first come into the world? I am bound to confess that it was first originated by Kant's Practical Reason with its Categorical Imperative. For when this Practical Reason had once been admitted, nothing further was needed than the addition of a second, no less sovereign Theoretical Reason, as its counterpart, or twin-sister: a Reason which proclaims metaphysical truths *ex tripode*. I have described the brilliant success of this invention in my Fundamental Problems of Ethics [1] to which work I refer my reader. Now, although I grant that Kant first gave rise to this false assumption, am, nevertheless, bound to add, that those who want to dance are not long in finding a piper. For it is surely as though a curse lay on mankind, causing them, in virtue of a natural affinity for all that is corrupt and bad, to prefer and hold up to admiration the inferior, not to say downright defective, portions of the works of eminent minds, while the really admirable parts are tolerated as merely accessory. Very few in our time know wherein the peculiar depth and true grandeur of Kant's philosophy lies; for his works have necessarily ceased to be comprehended since they have ceased to be studied. In fact, they are now only cursorily read, for historical purposes, by those who are under the delusion that philosophy has advanced, not to say begun, since Kant. We soon perceive therefore, that in spite of all their talk about Kantian philosophy, these people really know nothing of it but the husk, the mere outer envelope, and that if perchance they may here or there have caught up a stray sentence or brought away a rough sketch of it, they have never penetrated to the depths of its meaning and spirit. People of this sort have always been chiefly attracted, in Kant's Philosophy,

[1] Schopenhauer, "Die beiden Grundprobleme der Ethik," p. 148 and *sqq.* (p. 146 *et seq.* of 2nd edition.)

first of all by the Antinomies, on account of their oddity, but still more by his Practical Reason with its Categorical Imperative, nay even by the Moral Theory he placed on the top of it, though with this last he was never in earnest ; for a theoretical dogma which has only practical validity, is very like the wooden guns we allow our children to handle without fear of danger : properly speaking, it belongs to the same category as : "Wash my skin, but without wetting it." Now, as regards the Categorical Imperative, Kant never asserted it as a fact, but, on the contrary, protests repeatedly against this being done; he merely served it up as the result of an exceedingly curious combination of thoughts, because he stood in need of a sheet-anchor for morality. Our professors of philosophy, however, never sifted the matter to the bottom, so that it seems as if no one before me had ever thoroughly investigated it. Instead of this, they made all haste to bring the Categorical Imperative into credit as a firmly established fact, calling it in their purism "the moral law"—which, by the way, always reminds me of Bürger's "Mam'zelle Larègle; " indeed, they have made out of it something as massive as the stone tables of Moses, whose place it entirely takes, for them. Now in my Essay upon the Fundament of Morality, I have brought this same Practical Reason with its Categorical Imperative under the anatomical knife, and proved so clearly and conclusively that they never had any life or truth, that I should like to see the man who can refute me with reasons, and so help the Categorical Imperative honestly on its legs again. Meanwhile, our professors of philosophy do not allow themselves to be put out of countenance by this. They can no more dispense with their "moral law of practical Reason," as a convenient *deus ex machina* on which to found their morality, than with Free Will : both are essential points in their old woman's philosophy. No matter if

I have made an end of both, since, for them, both continue to exist, like deceased sovereigns who for political reasons are occasionally allowed to continue reigning for a few days after their death. These worthies simply pursue their tactics of old against my merciless demolition of those two antiquated fictions : silence, silence; and so they glide past noiselessly, feigning ignorance, to make the public believe that I and the like of me are not worth listening to. Well, to be sure, their philosophical calling comes to them from the ministry, while mine only comes from Nature. True, we may at last perhaps discover that these heroes act upon the same principle as that idealistic bird, the ostrich, which imagines that by closing its eyes it does away with the huntsman. Ah well! we must bide our time ; if the public can only be brought to take up meantime with the barren twaddle, the unbearably tiresome repetitions, the arbitrary constructions of the Absolute, and the infant-school morality of these gentlemen—say, till I am dead and they can trim up my works as they like—we shall then see.

Morgen habe denn das Rechte
Seine Freunde wohlgesinnet,
Wenn nur heute noch das Schlechte
Vollen Platz und Gunst gewinnet.
GÖTHE, *West-Oestlicher Divan.*

But do these gentlemen know what time of day it is? A long predicted epoch has set in ; the church is beginning to totter, nay it totters already to such a degree, that it is doubtful whether it will ever be able to recover its centre of gravity ; for faith is lost. The light of revelation, like other lights, requires a certain amount of darkness as an indispensable condition. The number of those who have been unfitted for belief by a certain degree and extent of knowledge, is already very large. Of this we have evident signs in the general diffusion of that shallow Rationalism which is showing its bulldog face daily more and more overtly. It quietly sets to work to measure those profound mysteries of Christianity over which centuries have brooded and disputed with its draper's ell, and thinks itself wondrous wise withal. It is, however, the very quintessence of Christianity, the dogma of Original Sin, which these shallow-brained Rationalists have especially singled out for a laughing-stock; precisely because nothing seems clearer or more certain to them, than that existence should begin for each of us with our birth: nothing therefore so impossible as that we can have come into the world already burdened with guilt. How acute! And just as in times of prevailing poverty and neglect, wolves begin to make their appearance in villages; so does Materialism, ever lying in wait, under these circumstances lift up its head and come to the front hand in hand with Bestialism, its companion, which some call Humanism. Our thirst after knowledge augments with our incapacity for belief. There comes a boiling-point in the scale of all intellectual development, at which all faith, all revelation, and all authority evaporate, and Man claims the right to judge for himself; the right, not only to be taught, but to be convinced. The leading-strings of his infancy have fallen off, and henceforth he demands leave to walk alone. Yet his craving for Metaphysics can no more be extinguished than any physical want. Then it is, that the desire for philosophy becomes serious and that mankind invokes the spirits of all the genuine thinkers who have issued from its ranks. Then, too, empty verbiage and the impotent endeavours of emasculated intellects no longer suffice; the want of a serious philosophy is felt, having other aims in view than fees and salaries, and caring little therefore whether it meets the approbation of cabinet-ministers, or councillors, whether it serves the purposes of this or that religious faction, or not; a philosophy which, on the contrary, clearly shows that it has a very different mission in view from that of procuring a livelihood for the poor in spirit.

But I return to my argument. By means of an amplification which only needed a little audacity, a *theoretical* oracle had been added to the *practical* oracle with which Kant had wrongly endowed Reason. The credit of this invention is no doubt due to F. H. Jacobi, from whom the professional philosophers joyfully and thankfully received the precious gift, as a means to help them out of the straits to which Kant had reduced them. That cool, calm, deliberate Reason, which Kant had criticized so mercilessly, was henceforth degraded to *Understanding* and known by this name; while Reason was supposed to denote an entirely imaginary, fictitious faculty, admitting us, as it were, to a little window overlooking the superlunar, nay, the supernatural world, through which all those truths are handed to us ready cut and dried, concerning which old-fashioned, honest, reflective Reason had for ages vainly argued and contended. And it is on such a mere product of the imagination, such a completely fictitious Reason as this, that German sham philosophy has been based for the last fifty years; first, as the free construction and projection of the absolute *Ego* and the emanation from it of the *non-Ego*; then, as the intellectual intuition of absolute identity or indifference, and its evolutions to Nature; or again, as the arising of God out of his dark depths or bottomless pit [1] *à la* Jakob Böhme; lastly, as the pure, self-thinking, absolute Idea, the scene of the balletdance of the self-moving conceptions—still, at the same time, always as immediate apprehension (*Vernehmen*) of the Divine, the supersensuous, the Deity, verity, beauty and as many other " -ties " as may be desired, or even as a mere

---

[1] " *Aus seinem Grund oder Ungrund.*"

vague presentiment[1] of all these wonders.—So this is Reason, is it? Oh no, it is simply a farce, of which our professors of philosophy, who are sorely perplexed by Kant's serious critiques, avail themselves in order to pass off the subjects of the established religion of their country somehow or other, *per fas aut nefas*, for the results of philosophy.

For it behoves all professorial philosophy, before all things, to establish beyond doubt, and to give a philosophical basis to, the doctrine, that there is a God, Creator, and Ruler of the Universe, a personal, consequently individual, Being, endowed with Understanding and Will, who has created the world out of nothing, and who rules it with sublime wisdom, power and goodness. This obligation, however, places our professors of philosophy in an awkward position with respect to serious philosophy. For Kant had appeared and the Critique of Pure Reason, was written more than sixty years ago, the result being, that of all the proofs of the existence of God which had been brought forward during the Christian ages, and which may be reduced to three which alone are possible, none are able to accomplish the desired end. Nay, the impossibity of any such proof, and with it the impossibility of all speculative theology, is shown at length *à priori* and not in the empty verbiage or Hegelian jargon now in fashion, which may be made to mean anything one likes, but quite seriously and honestly, in the good old-fashioned way ; wherefore, however little it may have been to the taste of many people, nothing cogent could be brought forward in reply to it for the last sixty years, and the proofs of the existence of God have in consequence lost all credit, and are no longer in use. Our professors of philosophy have even begun to look down upon them and treat them with decided contempt, as ridiculous and superfluous attempts to demonstrate what was self-evident.

[1] " *Ahnung* without the *d*."   See above, p. 133.   (Tr.'s note.)

Ho ! ho ! what a pity this was not found out sooner! How much trouble might have been spared in searching whole centuries for these proofs, and how needless it would have been for Kant to bring the whole weight of his Critique of Reason to bear upon and crush them ! Some folks, will no doubt be reminded by this contempt of the fox with the sour grapes. But those who wish to see a slight specimen of it will find a particularly characteristic one in Schelling's " Philosophische Schriften," vol. i., 1809, p. 152. Now, whilst others were consoling themselves with Kant's assertion, that it is just as impossible to prove the non-existence, as the existence, of God—as if, forsooth, the old wag did not know that *affirmanti incumbit probatio*— Jacobi's admirable invention came to the rescue of our perplexed professors, and granted German *savants* of this century a peculiar sort of Reason that had never been known or heard of before.

Yet all these artifices were quite unnecessary. For the impossibility of proving the existence of God by no means interferes with that existence, since it rests in unshakeable security on a much firmer basis. It is indeed a matter of revelation, and this is besides all the more certain, because that revelation was exclusively vouchsafed to a single people, called, on this account, the chosen people of God. This is made evident by the fact, that the notion of God, as personal Ruler and Creator of the world, ordaining everything for the best, is to be found in no other religion but the Jewish, and the two faiths derived from it, which might consequently in a wider sense be called Jewish sects. We find no trace of such a notion in any other religion, ancient or modern. For surely no one would dream of confounding this Creator God Almighty with the Hindoo Brahm, which is living in me, in you, in my horse, in your dog—or even with Brahma, who is born and dies to make way for other Brahmas, and to whom

moreover the production of the world is imputed as sin and
guilt[1]—least of all with beguiled Saturn's voluptuous son,
to whom Prometheus, defiant, prophesies his downfall. But
if we finally direct our attention towards the religion which
numbers most followers, and in this respect may therefore
be said to rank foremost : that is, Buddhism, we can
no longer shut our eyes to the fact that it is as decidedly
and explicitly atheistic, as it is idealistic and ascetic ; and
this moreover to such a degree, that its priests express
the greatest abhorrence of the doctrine of pure Theism
whenever it is brought to their notice. Therefore, in a
treatise handed to a Catholic bishop by the High Priest
of the Buddhists at Ava,[2] the doctrine " that there is a
Being who has created the world and all things, and who
alone is worthy of worship," is counted among the six
damnable heresies.[3] This is entirely corroborated by
I. J. Schmidt, a most excellent and learned authority,
whom I consider as having undoubtedly the deepest knowledge of Buddhism of any European *savant*, and who, in his
work " Upon the connection between Gnostic doctrines and
Buddhism," p. 9, says:—

"In the writings of the Buddhists not a trace is to be
found of any positive indication of a Supreme Being as the
principle of Creation. Whenever this subject presents
itself consistently in the course of argument, it seems,
indeed, to be intentionally evaded." And again: " The
system of Buddhism knows of no eternal, uncreated,

[1] "If Brimha be unceasingly employed in the creation of worlds . . . . .
how can tranquillity be obtained by inferior orders of being ? " Prabodh
Chandro Daya, translated by J. Taylor, p. 23.—Brahma is also part of
the Trimurti, which is the personification of nature, as procreation,
preservation, and death : that is, he represents the first of these.

[2] See " Asiatic Researches," vol. vi. p. 268, and Sangermano's " De-
scription of the Burmese Empire," p. 81.

[3] See I. J. Schmidt, " Forschungen im Gebiete der älteren Bildungs-
geschichte Mittelasiens." St. Petersburg, 1824, pp. 276, and 180.

one and only Being, having existed before Time and created all that is visible and invisible. This idea is quite foreign to Buddhism, and not a trace of it is to be found in Buddhist works. And just as little mention do we find of Creation. True, the visible Universe is not without a beginning, but it *arose* out of empty Space, according to consistent, immutable, natural laws. We should however err, were we to assume that anything—call it Fate or Nature— is regarded or revered by the Buddhists as a divine principle; on the contrary, it is just this very development of empty Space, this precipitate from it or this division into countless parts, this Matter thus arising, which constitutes the Evil of *Jirtintschi*, or of the Universe in its inner and outer relations, out of which sprang *Ortschilang*, or continuous change according to immutable laws, which the same Evil had established." Then again : [1] " The expression *Creation* is foreign to Buddhism, which only knows *Cosmogony ;* " and, " We must comprehend that no idea of a creation of divine origin is compatible with their system." I could bring forward a hundred corroborative passages like these ; but will limit myself to one more, which I quote on account of its popular and official character. The third volume of a very instructive Buddhist work, "Mahavansi, Raja-ratnacari, and Raja-Vali," [2] contains a translation of the interrogatories to which the High Priests of the five chief Pagodas were separately and successively subjected by the Dutch Governor of Ceylon about the year 1766. It is exceedingly amusing to see the contrast between the interlocutors, who have the greatest difficulty in understanding one another's meaning. In conformity with the doctrines of their faith, these priests, who are penetrated with love

[1] I. J. Schmidt, Lecture delivered in the Academy at St. Petersburg on the 15th Sept. 1830, p. 26.

[2] Mahavansi, Raja-ratnacari, and Raja-Vali, from the Singhalese, by E. Upham. London, 1833.

and compassion for all living beings, not excepting even
Dutch Governors, spare no pains to satisfy him by their
answers.   But the artless, naïve Atheism of these priests,
whose piety extends even to practising continence, soon comes
into conflict with the deep convictions founded on Judaism,
imbibed by the Governor in his infancy.   This faith has
become a second nature for him; he cannot in the least
understand that these priests are not Theists, therefore
he constantly returns to his inquiries after a Supreme
Being, asking them who created the world, and so forth.
Whereupon they answer that there can be no higher
being than Buddha Shakia-Muni, the Victorious and
the Perfect, who, though a king's son by birth, volun-
tarily lived the life of a beggar, and preached to the
end his sublime doctrine, for the Redemption of mankind,
and for our salvation from the misery of constant renascence.   They hold that the world has not been made by
anyone,[1] that it is self-created, that Nature spreads it out,
and draws it in again; but that it is that, which existing,
does not exist: that it is the necessary accompaniment of
renascence, and that renascence is the result of our sinful
conduct, &c. &c. &c.   I mention such facts as these chiefly
on account of the really scandalous way in which German
savants still universally persist, even to the present day, in
looking upon Religion and Theism as identical and synonymous; whereas Religion is, in fact, to Theism as the
genus to the single species, and Judaism and Theism are
alone identical.   For this reason we stigmatize as heathen
all nations who are neither Jews, Christians, nor Mahometans.   Christians are even taxed by Mahometans and Jews
with the impurity of their Theism, because of the dogma
of the Trinity.   For, whatever may be said to the contrary,

---

[1] Κόσμον τόνδε, φησὶν Ἡράκλειτος, οὔτε τις θεῶν οὔτε ἀνθρώπων
ἐποίησεν.   (Neither a God nor a man created this world, says Hera-
clitus.)   Plut. " De animæ procreatione," c. 5.

Christianity has Indian blood in its veins, therefore it constantly tends to free itself from Judaism. The Critique of Pure Reason is the most serious attack that has ever been made upon Theism—and this is why our professors of philosophy have been in such a hurry to set Kant aside; but had that work appeared in any country where Buddhism prevailed, it would simply have been regarded as an edifying treatise intended to refute heresy more thoroughly by a salutary confirmation of the orthodox doctrine of Idealism—that is, the doctrine of the merely apparent existence of the world, as it presents itself to our senses. Even the two other religions which coexist with Buddhism in China—those of Taotsee and of Confucius—are just as Atheistic as Buddhism itself; wherefore the missionaries have never been able to translate the first verse of the Pentateuch into Chinese, because there is no word in the language for God and Creation. Even the missionary Gützlaff, in his "History of the Chinese Empire," p. 18, has the honesty to say: "It is extraordinary that none of the (Chinese) philosophers ever soared high enough to reach the knowledge of a Creator and Lord of the Universe, although they possessed the Light of Nature in full measure." J. F. Davis likewise quotes a passage, which is quite in accordance with this, from Milne's Preface to his translation of the Shing-yu, where in speaking of that work, he says that we may see from it "that the bare Light of Nature, as it is called, even when aided by all the light of Pagan philosophy, is totally incapable of leading men to the knowledge and worship of the true God." All this confirms the fact that revelation is the sole foundation on which Theism rests; indeed, it must be so, unless revelation is to be superfluous. This is a good opportunity for observing that the word Atheism itself implies a surreptitious assumption, since it takes Theism for granted as a matter of course. It would be more honest to say

Non-Judaism instead of Atheism, and Non-Jew instead of Atheist.

Now as, according to the above, the existence of God belongs to revelation, by which it is firmly established, it has no need whatever of human authentication. Philosophy, however, is properly speaking only an idle, superfluous attempt to let Reason—that is, the human power of thinking, reflecting, deliberating—once in a while, try its own powers unassisted, as a child is now and then allowed to run alone on a lawn and try its strength without leading-strings, just to see what will come of it. Tests and experiments of this kind we call *speculation*; and it lies in the nature of the matter that it should, for once, leave all authority, human or divine, out of consideration, ignore it, and go its own way in search of the most sublime, most important truths. Now, if on this basis it should arrive at the very same results as those mentioned above, to which Kant had come, speculation has no right on that account to cast all honesty and conscience forthwith aside, and take to by-ways, in order somehow or other to get back to the domain of Judaism, as its *conditio sine qua non*; it ought rather henceforth to seek truth quite honestly and simply by any road that may happen to lie open before it, but never to allow any other light than that of Reason to guide it: thus advancing calmly and confidently, like one at work in his vocation, without concern as to where that road may lead.

If our professors of philosophy put a different construction on the matter, and hold that they cannot eat their bread in honour, so long as they have not reinstalled God Almighty on his throne—as if, forsooth, he stood in need of *them*—this already accounts for their not relishing my writings, and explains why I am not the man for them; for I certainly do not deal in this sort of article, nor have I the newest reports to communicate about the Almighty every Leipzig fair-time, as they have.

CHAPTER VI.

ON THE THIRD CLASS OF OBJECTS FOR THE SUBJECT AND
THAT FORM OF THE PRINCIPLE OF SUFFICIENT REASON
WHICH PREDOMINATES IN IT.

§ 35. *Explanation of this Class of Objects.*

IT is the formal part of complete representations—that is to say, the intuitions given us *à priori* of the forms of the outer and inner sense, *i.e.* of Space and of Time— which constitutes the Third Class of Objects for our representative faculty.

As pure intuitions, these forms are objects for the faculty of representation by themselves and apart from complete representations and from the determinations of being empty or filled which these representations first add to them ; since even pure points and pure lines cannot be brought to sensuous perception, but are only *à priori* intuitions, just as the infinite expansion and the infinite divisibility of Space and of Time are exclusively objects of pure intuition and foreign to empirical perception. That which distinguishes the third class of representations, in which Space and Time are *pure intuitions*, from the first class, in which they are *sensuously* (and moreover conjointly) *perceived,* is Matter, which I have therefore defined, on the one hand, as the perceptibility of Space and Time, on the other, as objectified Causality.

The form of Causality, on the contrary, which belongs to the Understanding, is not separately and by itself an object for our faculty of representation, nor have we consciousness of it, until it is connected with what is material in our knowledge.

§ 36. *Principle of the Sufficient Reason of Being.*

Space and Time are so constituted, that all their parts stand in mutual relation, so that each of them conditions and is conditioned by another. We call this relation in Space, *position ;* in Time, *succession.* These relations are peculiar ones, differing entirely from all other possible relations of our representations ; neither the Understanding nor the Reason are therefore able to grasp them by means of mere conceptions, and pure intuition *à priori* alone makes them intelligible to us ; for it is impossible by mere conceptions to explain clearly what is meant by above and below, right and left, behind and before, before and after. Kant rightly confirms this by the assertion, that the distinction between our right and left glove cannot be made intelligible in any other way than by intuition. Now, the law by which the divisions of Space and of Time determine one another reciprocally with reference to these relations (position and succession) is what I call the *Principle of the Sufficient Reason of Being, principium rationis sufficientis essendi.* I have already given an example of this relation in § 15, by which I have shown, through the connection between the sides and angles of a triangle, that this relation is not only quite different from that between cause and effect, but also from that between reason of knowledge and consequent ; wherefore here the condition may be called *Reason of Being, ratio essendi.* The insight into such a *reason of being* can, of course, become a reason of knowing : just as the insight into the law of causality and its application to a particular case is the reason of knowledge of the effect ; but this in no way annuls the complete distinction between Reason of Being, Reason of Becoming, and Reason of Knowing. It often happens, that what according to *one* form of our principle is *consequence*, is, according to another, *reason*. The rising of the quicksilver in a thermometer, for instance, is the *consequence* of increased heat according to the law of causality, while according to the principle of the sufficient reason of knowing it is the *reason*, the ground of knowledge, of the increased heat and also of the judgment by which this is asserted.

§ 37. *Reason of Being in Space.*

The position of each division of Space towards any other, say of any given line—and this is equally applicable to planes, bodies, and points—determines also absolutely its totally different position with reference to any other possible line ; so that the latter position stands to the former in the relation of the consequent to its reason. As the position of this given line towards any other possible line likewise determines its position towards all the others, and as therefore the position of the first two lines is itself determined by all the others, it is immaterial which we consider as being first determined and determining the others, *i.e.* which particular one we regard as *ratio* and which others as *rationata*. This is so, because in Space there is no succession ; for it is precisely by uniting Space and Time to form the collective representation of the complex of experience, that the representation of coexistence arises. Thus an analogue to so-called reciprocity prevails everywhere in the Reason of Being in Space, as we shall see in § 48, where I enter more fully into the reciprocity of reasons. Now, as every line is determined by all the others just as much as it determines them, it is arbitrary to consider any line merely as determining and not as being determined, and the position of each towards any other admits the question as to its position with reference to some other line, which second position necessarily determines the first and makes it that which it is. It is therefore just as impossible to find an end *a parte ante* in the series of links in the chain of Reasons of Being as in that of Reasons of Becoming, nor can we find any *a parte post* either, because of the infinity of Space and of the lines possible within Space. All possible relative spaces are figures, because they are limited; and all these figures have their Reason of Being in one another, because they are conterminous. The *series rationum essendi* in Space therefore, like the *series rationum fiendi*, proceeds *in infinitum*; and moreover not only in a single direction, like the latter, but in all directions.

Nothing of all this can be proved; for the truth of these principles is transcendental, they being directly founded upon the intuition of Space given us *à priori*.

§ 38. *Reason of being in Time. Arithmetic.*

Every instant in Time is conditioned by the preceding one. The Sufficient Reason of Being, as the law of consequence, is so simple here, because Time has only one dimension, therefore it admits of no multiplicity of relations. Each instant is conditioned by its predecessor; we can only reach it through that predecessor: only so far as this *was* and has elapsed, does the present one exist. All counting rests upon this nexus of the divisions of Time, numbers only serving to mark the single steps in the succession; upon it therefore rests all arithmetic likewise, which teaches absolutely nothing but methodical abbreviations of numeration. Each number pre-supposes its predecessors as the reasons of its being: we can only reach the number *ten* by passing through all the preceding numbers, and it is only in virtue of this insight that I know, that where ten are, there also are eight, six, four.

§ 39. *Geometry.*

The whole science of Geometry likewise rests upon the nexus of the position of the divisions of Space. It would, accordingly, be an insight into that nexus; only such an insight being, as we have already said, impossible by means of mere conceptions, or indeed in any other way than by intuition, every geometrical proposition would have to be brought back to sensuous intuition, and the proof would simply consist in making the particular nexus in question clear; nothing more could be done. Nevertheless we find Geometry treated quite differently. Euclid's Twelve Axioms are alone held to be based upon mere intuition, and even of these only the Ninth, Eleventh, and Twelfth are properly speaking admitted to be founded upon different, separate intuitions; while the rest are supposed to be founded upon the knowledge that in science we do not, as in experience, deal with real things existing for themselves side by side, and susceptible of endless variety, but on the contrary with conceptions, and in Mathematics with *normal intuitions,* i.e. figures and numbers, whose laws are binding for all experience, and which therefore combine the comprehensiveness of the conception with the complete definiteness of the single representation. For although, as intuitive representations, they are throughout determined with complete precision—no room being left in *this* way by anything remaining undetermined—still they are general, because they are the bare forms of all phenomena, and, as such, applicable to all real objects to which such forms belong, What Plato says of his Ideas would therefore, even in Geometry, hold good of these normal intuitions, just as well as of conceptions, *i.e.* that two cannot be exactly

similar, for then they would be but one.[1] This would, I
say, be applicable also to normal intuitions in Geometry,
if it were not that, as exclusively spacial objects, these
differ from one another in mere juxtaposition, that is, in
place. Plato had long ago remarked this, as we are told
by Aristotle:[2] ἔτι δὲ, παρὰ τὰ αἰσθητὰ καὶ τὰ εἴδη, τὰ μαθη-
ματικὰ τῶν πραγμάτων εἶναί φησι μεταξύ, διαφέροντα τῶν μὲν
αἰσθητῶν τῷ ἀίδια καὶ ἀκίνητα εἶναι, τῶν δὲ εἰδῶν τῷ τὰ μὲν
πόλλ᾽ ἄττα ὅμοια εἶναι, τὸ δὲ εἶδος αὐτὸ ἓν ἕκαστον μόνον
(item, præter sensibilia et species, mathematica rerum ait
media esse, a sensibilibus quidem differentia eo, quod per-
petua et immobilia sunt, a speciebus vero eo, quod illorum
quidem multa quædam similia sunt, species vero ipsa
unaquæque sola). Now the mere knowledge that such a
difference of place does not annul the rest of the identity,
might surely, it seems to me, supersede the other nine
axioms, and would, I think, be better suited to the nature
of science, whose aim is knowledge of the particular through
the general, than the statement of nine separate axioms
all based upon the same insight. Moreover, what Aristotle
says: ἐν τούτοις ἡ ἰσότης ἐνότης (in illis æqualitas unitas
est)[3] then becomes applicable to geometrical figures.

But with reference to the normal intuitions in Time, i.e.

---

[1] Platonic ideas may, after all, be described as normal intuitions,
which would hold good not only for what is formal, but also for what is
material in complete representations—therefore as complete representations which, as such, would be determined throughout, while compre-
hending many things at once, like conceptions : that is to say, as representatives of conceptions, but which are quite adequate to those
conceptions, as I have explained in § 28.

[2] Aristot. "Metaph." i. 6, with which compare x. 1. "Further, says
he, besides things sensible and the ideas, there are things mathematical
coming in between the two, which differ from the things sensible, inasmuch as they are eternal and immovable, and from the ideas, inasmuch
as many of them are like each other ; but the idea is absolutely and
only one." (Tr.'s Add.)

[3] "In these it is equality that constitutes unity." (Tr.'s Add.)

to numbers, even this distinction of juxtaposition no longer
exists. Here, as with conceptions, absolutely nothing but the
identitas indiscernibilium remains : for there is but one five
and one seven. And in this we may perhaps also find a reason
why 7 + 5 = 12 is a synthetical proposition *à priori,*
founded upon intuition, as Kant profoundly discovered,
and not an identical one, as it is called by Herder in his
" Metakritik " . 12 = 12 is an identical proposition.

In Geometry, it is therefore only in dealing with axioms
that we appeal to intuition. All the other theorems are
demonstrated : that is to say, a reason of knowing is given,
the truth of which everyone is bound to acknowledge.
The logical truth of the theorem is thus shown, but not its
transcendental truth (v. §§ 30 and 32), which, as it lies in
the reason of *being* and not in the reason of *knowing,*
never can become evident excepting by means of intuition.
This explains why this sort of geometrical demonstration,
while it no doubt conveys the conviction that the theorem
which has been demonstrated is true, nevertheless gives no
insight as to *why* that which it asserts is what it is. In
other words, we have not found its Reason of Being ; but
the desire to find it is usually then thoroughly roused.
For proof by indicating the reason of knowledge only
effects conviction (*convictio*), not knowledge (*cognitio*) : therefore it might perhaps be more correctly called *elenchus*
than *demonstratio.* This is why, in most cases, therefore, it
leaves behind it that disagreeable feeling which is given
by all want of insight, when perceived ; and here, the
want of knowledge *why* a thing is as it is, makes itself all
the more keenly felt, because of the certainty just attained,
that it is as it is. This impression is very much like the
feeling we have, when something has been conjured into or
out of our pocket, and we cannot conceive how. The
reason of knowing which, in such demonstrations as
these, is given without the reason of being, resembles

certain physical theories, which present the phenomenon without being able to indicate its cause: for instance, Leidenfrost's experiment, inasmuch as it succeeds also in a platina crucible; whereas the reason of being of a geometrical proposition which is discovered by intuition, like every knowledge we acquire, produces satisfaction. When once the reason of being is found, we base our conviction of the truth of the theorem upon that reason alone, and no longer upon the reason of knowing given us by the demonstration. Let us, for instance, take the sixth proposition of the first Book of Euclid :—

"If two angles of a triangle are equal, the sides also

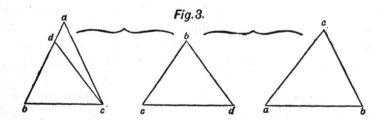

Fig. 3.

which subtend, or are opposite to, the equal angles shall be equal to one another." (See fig. 3.)

Which Euclid demonstrates as follows :—

"Let $a\,b\,c$ be a triangle having the angle $a\,b\,c$ equal to the angle $a\,c\,b$, then the side $a\,c$ must be equal to the side $a\,b$ also.

"For, if side $a\,b$ be not equal to side $a\,c$, one of them is greater than the other. Let $a\,b$ be greater than $a\,c$; and from $b\,a$ cut off $b\,d$ equal to $c\,a$, and draw $d\,c$. Then, in the triangles $d\,b\,c$, $a\,b\,c$, because $d\,b$ is equal to $a\,c$, and $b\,c$ is common to both triangles, the two sides $d\,b$ and $b\,c$ are equal to the two sides $a\,c$, $a\,b$, each to each; and the angle $d\,b\,c$ is equal to the angle $a\,c\,b$, therefore the base $d\,c$ is equal to the base $a\,b$, and the triangle $d\,b\,c$ is equal to the triangle *a b c*, the less triangle equal to the greater,—which is absurd.   Therefore *a b* is not unequal to *a c*, that is, *a b* is equal to *a c*."

Now, in this demonstration we have a reason of know-ing for the truth of the proposition.   But who bases his conviction of that geometrical truth upon this proof? Do we not rather base our conviction upon the reason of being, which we know intuitively, and according to which (by a necessity which admits of no further demonstration, but only of evidence through intuition) two lines drawn from both extreme ends of another line, and inclining equally towards each other, can only meet at a point which is equally distant from both extremities;   since the two arising angles are properly but one, to which the opposite-ness of position gives the appearance of being two ;   where-fore there is no reason why the lines should meet at any point nearer to the one end than to the other.

It is the knowledge of the reason of being which shows us the necessary consequence of the conditioned from its condition—in this instance, the lateral equality from the angular equality—that is, it shows their connection; whereas the reason of knowing only shows their coexistence.   Nay, we might even maintain that the usual method of proving merely convinces us of their coexistence in the actual figure given us as an example, but by no means that they are always coexistent;   for, as the necessary con-nection is not shown, the conviction we acquire of this truth rests simply upon induction, and is based upon the fact, that we find it is so in every figure we make. The reason of being is certainly not as evident in all cases as it is in simple theorems like this 6th one of Euclid ; still I am persuaded that it might be brought to evidence in every theorem, however complicated, and that the proposi-tion can always be reduced to some such simple intuition. Besides, we are all just as conscious *à priori* of the necessity of such a reason of being for each relation of Space, as we are of the necessity of a cause for each change. In complicated theorems it will, of course, be very difficult to show that reason of being; and this is not the place for difficult geometrical researches. Therefore, to make my meaning somewhat clearer, I will now try to bring back to its reason of being a moderately complicated proposition, in which nevertheless that reason is not immediately evident. Passing over the intermediate theorems, I take the 16th:

"In every triangle in which one side has been produced, the exterior angle is greater than either of the interior opposite angles."

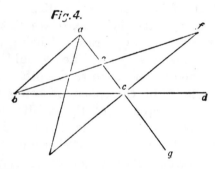

Fig. 4.

This Euclid demonstrates in the following manner (see fig. 4) :—

"Let $a\,b\,c$ be a triangle ; and let the side $b\,c$ be produced to d; then the exterior angle $a\,c\,d$ shall be greater than either of the interior opposite angles $b\,a\,c$ or $c\,b\,a$. Bisect the side $a\,c$ at e, and join $b\,e$; produce $b\,e$ to f, making $e\,f$ equal to $e\,b$, and join $f\,c$. Produce $a\,c$ to g. Because $a\,e$ is equal to $e\,c$, and $b\,e$ to $e\,f$; the two sides $a\,e, e\,b$, are equal to the two sides $c\,e, e\,f$, each to each ; and the angle $a\,e\,b$ is equal to the angle $c\,e\,f$, because they are opposite vertical angles ; therefore the base $a\,b$ is equal to the base $c\,f$, and the triangle $a\,e\,b$ is equal to the triangle $c\,e\,f$, and the remaining angles of one triangle to the remaining angles of the other, each to each, to which the equal sides are opposite; therefore the angle *b a e* is equal to the angle *e c f*. But the angle *e c d* is greater than the angle *e c f*. Therefore the angle *a c d* is greater than the angle *a b c*."

" In the same manner, if the side *b c* be bisected, and the side *a c* be produced to *g*, it may be demonstrated that the angle *b c g*, that is, the opposite vertical angle *a c d* is greater than the angle *a b c*."

My demonstration of the same proposition would be as follows (see fig. 5) :—

For the angle *b a c* to be even equal to, let alone greater than, the angle *a c d*, the line *b a* toward *c a* would have to lie in the same direction as *b d* (for this is precisely what is meant by equality of the angles), *i.e.*, it must be parallel

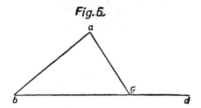

Fig. 5.

with *b d*; that is to say, *b a* and *b d* must never meet; but in order to form a triangle they must meet (reason of being), and must thus do the contrary of that which would be required for the angle *b a c* to be of the same size as the angle *a c d*.

For the angle *a b c* to be even equal to, let alone greater than, the angle *a c d*, line *b a* must lie in the same direction towards *b d* as *a c* (for this is what is meant by equality of the angles), *i.e.*, it must be parallel with *a c*, that is to say, *b a* and *a c* must never meet; but in order to form a triangle *b a* and *a c* must meet and must thus do the contrary of that which would be required for the angle *a b c* to be of the same size as *a c d*.

By all this I do not mean to suggest the introduction of

a new method of mathematical demonstration, nor the
substitution of my own proof for that of Euclid, for which
its whole nature unfits it, as well as the fact that it presupposes the conception of parallel lines, which in Euclid
comes much later. I merely wished to show what the
reason of being is, and wherein lies the difference between
it and the reason of knowing, which latter only effects *convictio,* a thing that differs entirely from insight into the
reason of being. The fact that Geometry only aims at
effecting *convictio,* and that this, as I have said, leaves
behind it a disagreeable impression, but gives no insight
into the reason of being—which insight, like all knowledge,

Fig.6.

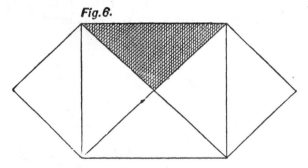

is satisfactory and pleasing—may perhaps be one of the
reasons for the great dislike which many otherwise eminent
heads have for mathematics.

I cannot resist again giving fig. 6, although it has already
been presented elsewhere; because the mere sight of it
without words conveys ten times more persuasion of the
truth of the Pythagorean theorem than Euclid's mouse-
trap demonstration.

Those readers for whom this chapter may have a special
interest will find the subject of it more fully treated in my
chief work, "Die Welt als Wille und Vorstellung," vol. i.
§ 15; vol. ii. chap. 13.

CHAPTER VII.

ON THE FOURTH CLASS OF OBJECTS FOR THE SUBJECT,
AND THE FORM OF THE PRINCIPLE OF SUFFICIENT
REASON WHICH PREDOMINATES IN IT.

§ 40. *General Explanation.*

THE last Class of Objects for our representative faculty
which remains to be examined is a peculiar but
highly important one. It comprises but *one* object for
each individual: that is, the immediate object of the inner
sense, the *Subject in volition*, which is Object for the Knowing Subject; wherefore it manifests itself in Time alone,
never in Space, and as we shall see, even in Time under an
important restriction.

§ 41. *Subject of Knowledge and Object.*

All knowledge presupposes Subject and Object. Even
self-consciousness (*Selbstbewusstsein*) therefore is not absolutely simple, but, like our consciousness of all other
things (*i.e.*, the faculty of perception), it is subdivided into
that which is known and that which knows. Now, that
which is known manifests itself absolutely and exclusively
as *Will*.

The Subject accordingly knows itself exclusively as
willing, but not as *knowing*. For the *ego* which represents, never can itself become representation or Object,
since it conditions all representations as their necessary

correlate; rather may the following beautiful passage·
from the Sacred Upanishad be applied to it: *Id videndum·*
non est: omnia videt; et id audiendum non est: omnia·
audit; sciendum non est: omnia scit: et intelligendum non
est: omnia intelligit. Præter id, videns, et sciens, et
audiens, et intelligens ens aliud non est.[1]

There can therefore be no *knowledge of knowing,* because
this would imply separation of the Subject from knowing,
while it nevertheless knew that knowing—which is impossible.

My answer to the objection, "I not only know, but
know also that I know," would be, "Your knowing that
you know only differs in words from your knowing. 'I
know that I know' means nothing more than 'I know,'
and this again, unless it is further determined, means·
nothing more than '*ego.*' If your knowing and your
knowing that you know are two different things, just try
to separate them, and first to know without knowing that
you know, then to know that you know without this
knowledge being at the same time knowing." No doubt,·
by leaving all *special* knowing out of the question, we may
at last arrive at the proposition "*I know*"—the last abstraction we are able to make; but this proposition is.
identical with "*Objects exist for me,*" and this again is·
identical with "*I am Subject,*" in which nothing more is
contained than in the bare word "*I.*"

Now, it may still be asked how the various cognitive·
faculties belonging to the Subject, such as Sensibility,·
Understanding, Reason, are known to us, if we do not
know the Subject. It is not through our knowing having
become an Object for us that these faculties are known to·
us, for then there would not be so many conflicting judgments concerning them; they are inferred rather, or

[1] "Oupnekhat," vol. i. p. 202.

more correctly, they are general expressions for the established classes of representations which, at all times, have
been more or less clearly distinguished in those cognitive
faculties. But, with reference to the necessary correlate
of these representations as their condition, *i.e.*, the Subject, these faculties are abstracted from them (the representations), and stand consequently towards the classes
of representations in precisely the same relation as the
Subject in general towards the Object in general. Now,
just as the Object is at once posited with the Subject (for
the word itself would otherwise have no meaning), and
conversely, as the Subject is at once posited with the
Object—so that being the Subject means exactly as much
as having an Object, and being an Object means the same
thing as being known by the Subject—so likewise, when
an Object is assumed as being determined *in any particular way*, do we also assume that the Subject *knows
precisely in that particular way.* So far therefore it is
immaterial whether we say that Objects have such and
such peculiar inherent determinations, or that the Subject
knows in such and such ways. It is indifferent whether
we say that Objects are divided into such and such classes,
or that such and such different cognitive faculties are
peculiar to the Subject. In that singular compound of
depth and superficiality, Aristotle, are to be found traces
even of insight into this truth, and indeed the critical
philosophy lies in embryo in his works. He says: [1]
ἡ ψυχὴ τὰ ὄντα πώς ἐστι πάντα (*anima quammodo est uni-
versa, quæ sunt*). And again: ὁ νοῦς ἐστι εἶδος εἰδῶν, *i.e.*,
the understanding is the form of forms, καὶ ἡ αἴσθησις
εἶδος αἰσθητῶν, and sensibility the form of sensuous
objects. Accordingly, it is all one whether we say, " sensibility and understanding are no more ;" or, " the world is

-----

[1] Aristot., "De anima," iii. 8.   " In a certain sense the intellect is all
that exists." (Tr.'s Add.)

at an end." It comes to the same thing whether we say,
"There are no conceptions," or "Reason is gone and
animals alone remain."

The dispute between Realism and Idealism, which appeared for the last time in the dispute between the Dog-
matists and Kantians, or between Ontology and Metaphysics on the one hand and Transcendental Æsthetic
and Transcendental Logic on the other, arose out of the
misapprehension of this relation and was based upon its
misapprehension with reference to the First and Third
Classes of representations as established by me, just as
the mediæval dispute between Realists and Nominalists
rested upon the misapprehension of this relation with
reference to the Second Class.

§ 42. *The Subject of Volition.*

According to what has preceded, the Subject of knowledge can never be known; it can never become Object or
representation. Nevertheless, as we have not only an
outer self-knowledge (in sensuous perception), but an inner
one also; and as, on the other hand, every knowledge, by
its very nature, presupposes a knower and a known, what
is known within us as such, is not the knower, but the
willer, the Subject of Volition: the Will. Starting from
knowledge, we may assert that "I know" is an analytical,
"I will," on the contrary, a synthetical, and moreover an
à posteriori proposition, that is, it is given by experience—
in this case by inner experience (*i.e.*, in Time alone). In
so far therefore the Subject of volition would be an
Object for us. Introspection always shows us to ourselves
as *willing*. In this *willing*, however, there are numerous
degrees, from the faintest wish to passion, and I have
often shown [1] that not only all our emotions, but even all

---

[1] See "Die beiden Grundprobleme der Ethik," p. 11, and in several
other places.

those movements of our inner man, which are subsumed under the wide conception of feeling, are states of the will.

Now, the identity of the willing with the knowing Subject, in virtue of which the word "I" includes and designates both, is the *nodus* [1] of the Universe, and therefore inexplicable. For we can only comprehend relations between Objects; but two Objects never can be one, excepting as parts of a whole. Here, where the Subject is in question, the rules by which we know Objects are no longer applicable, and actual identity of the knower with what is known as willing—that is, of Subject and Object—is *immediately given*. Now, whoever has clearly realized the utter impossibility of explaining this identity, will surely concur with me in calling it the miracle κατ᾽ εζοχήν.

Just as the Understanding is the subjective correlate to our First Class of representations, the Reason to the Second, and pure Sensibility to the Third, so do we find that the correlate to this Fourth Class is the inner sense, or Self-consciousness in general.

§ 43. *Willing. The Law of Motives (Motivation).*

It is just because the willing Subject is immediately given in self-consciousness, that we are unable further to define or to describe what willing is; properly speaking, it is the most direct knowledge we have, nay, one whose immediateness must finally throw light upon every other knowledge, as being very mediate.

At every resolution that we take ourselves, or that we see others take, we deem ourselves justified in asking, why? That is, we assume that something must have previously occurred, from which this resolution has resulted,

---

[1] *Weltknoten.*

and we call this something its reason, or, more correctly, the motive of the action which now follows. Without such a reason or motive, the action is just as inconceivable for us, as the movement of a lifeless body without being pushed or pulled. Motives therefore belong to causes, and have also been already numbered and characterized among them in § 20, as the third form of Causality. But all Causality is only the form of the Principle of Sufficient Reason in the First Class of Objects : that is, in the corporeal world given us in external perception. There it forms the link which connects changes one with another, the cause being that which, coming from outside, conditions each occurrence. The inner nature of such occurrences on the contrary continues to be a mystery for us : for we always remain on the outside. We certainly see this cause necessarily produce that effect ; but we do not learn how it is actually enabled to do so, or what is going on inside. Thus we see mechanical, physical, chemical effects, as well as those brought about by *stimuli*, in each instance follow from their respective causes without on that account ever completely understanding the process, the essential part of which remains a mystery for us; so we attribute it to qualities of bodies, to forces of Nature, or to vital energy, which, however, are all *qualitates occultæ*. Nor should we be at all better off as to comprehension of the movements and actions of animals and of human beings, which would also appear to us as induced in some unaccountable way by their causes (motives), were it not that here we are granted an insight into the inward part of the process ; we know, that is, by our own inward experience, that this is an act of the will called forth by the motive, which consists in a mere representation. Thus the effect produced by the motive, unlike that produced by all other causes, is not only known by us from outside, in a merely indirect way, but at the same time from inside, quite directly, and therefore according to its whole mode of action. Here we stand as it were behind the scenes, and learn the secret of the process by which cause produces effect in its most inward nature; for here our knowledge comes to us through a totally different channel and in a totally different way. From this results the important proposition : *The action of motives (motivation) is causality seen from within.* Here accordingly causality presents itself in quite a different way, in quite a different medium, and for quite another kind of knowledge ; therefore it must now be exhibited as a special and peculiar form of our principle, which consequently here presents itself as the Principle of the Sufficient Reason of Acting, *principium rationis sufficientis agendi*, or, more briefly, as the *Law of Motives (Law of Motivation)*.

As a clue to my philosophy in general, I here add, that this Fourth Class of Objects for the Subject, that is, the one object contained in it, the *will* which we apprehend within us, stands in the same relation towards the First Class as the law of motives towards the law of causality, as I have established it in § 20. This truth is the corner-stone of my whole Metaphysic.

As to the way in which, and the necessity with which, motives act, and as to the dependence of their action upon empirical, individual character, and even upon individual capacity for knowledge, &c. &c., I refer my readers to my Prize-essay on the Freedom of the Will, in which I have treated all this more fully.

§ 44. *Influence of the Will over the Intellect.*

It is not upon causality proper, but upon the identity of the knowing with the willing Subject, as shown in § 42, that the influence is based, which the will exercises over the intellect, when it obliges it to repeat representations that have once been present to it, and in general to turn its attention in this or that direction and evoke at pleasure any particular series of thoughts. And even in this, the will is determined by the law of motives, in accordance with which it also secretly rules what is called the association of ideas, to which I have devoted a separate chapter (the 14th) in the second volume of my chief work. This association of ideas is itself nothing but the application of the Principle of Sufficient Reason in its four forms to the subjective train of thought; that is, to the presence of representations in our consciousness. But it is the will of the individual that sets the whole mechanism in motion, by urging the intellect, in accordance with the interest, *i.e.*, the individual aims, of the person, to recall, together with its present representations, those which either logically or analogically, or by proximity in Time or Space, are nearly related to them. The will's activity in this, however, is so immediate, that in most cases we have no clear consciousness of it ; and so rapid, that we are at times even unconscious of the occasion which has thus called forth a representation. In such cases, it appears as if something had come into our consciousness quite independently of all connection with anything else ; that this, however, is impossible, is precisely the Root of the Principle of Sufficient Reason, which has been fully explained in the above-mentioned chapter of my chief work.[1] Every picture which suddenly presents itself to our imagination, every judgment even that does not follow its previously present reason, must be called forth by an act of volition having a motive; although that motive may often escape our perception owing to its insignificance, and although such acts of volition are often in like manner unperceived, because they

---

[1] See "Die Welt, a. W. u. V." vol. ii. ch. xiv.

take place so easily, that wish and fulfilment are simultaneous.

§ 45. *Memory.*

That peculiar faculty of the knowing Subject which enables it to obey the will the more readily in repeating representations, the oftener they have already been present to it—in other words, its capacity for being exercised—is what we call *Memory.* I cannot agree with the customary view, by which it is looked upon as a sort of store-house in which we keep a stock of ready-made representations always at our disposal, only without being always conscious of their possession. The voluntary repetition of representations which have once been present becomes so easy through practice, that one link in a series of representations no sooner becomes present to us, than we at once evoke all the rest, often even, as it were, involuntarily. If we were to look for a metaphor for this characteristic quality of our representative faculty (such as that of Plato, who compared it with a soft mass that receives and retains impressions), I think the best would be that of a piece of drapery, which, after having been repeatedly folded in the same folds, at last falls into them, as it were, of its own accord. The body learns by practice to obey the will, and the faculty of representing does precisely the same. A remembrance is not by any means, as the usual view supposes, always the same representation which is, as it were, fetched over and over again from its store-house; a new one, on the contrary, arises each time, only practice makes this especially easy. Thus it comes to pass that pictures of our imagination, which we fancy we have stowed away in our memory, become imperceptibly modified: a thing which we realize when we see some familiar object again after a long time, and find that it no longer completely corresponds to the image we bring with us. This could not be if we retained ready-made representations. It is just for this reason too, that acquired knowledge, if left unexercised, gradually fades from our memory, precisely because it was the result of practice coming from habit and knack; thus most scholars, for instance, forget their Greek, and most artists their Italian on their return from Italy. This is also why we find so much difficulty in recalling to mind a name or a line of poetry formerly familiar to us, when we have ceased to think of it for several years; whereas when once we succeed in remembering it, we have it again at our disposal for some time, because the practice has been renewed. Everyone therefore who knows several languages, will do well to make a point of reading occasionally in each, that he may ensure to himself their possession.

This likewise explains why the surroundings and events of our childhood impress themselves so deeply on our memory; it is because, in childhood we have but few, and those chiefly intuitive, representations: so that we are induced to repeat them constantly for the sake of occupation. People who have little capability for original thought do this all their lives (and moreover not only with intuitive representations, but with conceptions and words also); sometimes therefore they have remarkably good memories, when obtuseness and sluggishness of intellect do not act as impediments. Men of genius, on the contrary, are not always endowed with the best of memories, as, for instance, Rousseau has told us of himself. Perhaps this may be accounted for by their great abundance of new thoughts and combinations, which leaves them no time for frequent repetition. Still, on the whole, genius is seldom found with a very bad memory; because here a greater energy and mobility of the whole thinking faculty makes up for the want of constant practice. Nor must we forget that Mnemosyne was the mother of the Muses. We may accordingly say, that our memory stands under two contending influences, that of the energy of the representative faculty on the one hand, and that of the quantity of representations occupying that faculty on the other.   The less energy there is in the faculty, the fewer must be the representations, and conversely.   This explains the impaired memory of habitual novel-readers, for it is with them as with men of genius : the multitude of representations following rapidly upon each other, leaves no time or patience for repetition and practice ;   only, in novels, these representations are not the readers' own, but other people's thoughts and combinations quickly succeeding each other, and the readers themselves are wanting in that which, in genius, counterbalances repetition.   The whole thing besides is subject to the corrective, that we all have most memory for that which interests us, and least for that which does not.   Great minds therefore are apt to forget in an incredibly short time the petty affairs and trifling occurrences of daily life and the commonplace people with whom they come in contact, whereas they have a wonderful recollection of those things which have importance in themselves and for them.

It is, however, on the whole, easy to understand that we should more readily remember such series of representations as are connected together by the thread of one or more of the above-mentioned species of reasons and consequences, than such as have no connection with one another, but only with our will according to the law of motives ;   that is to say, those which are arbitrarily grouped.   For, in the former, the fact that we know the formal part *à priori*, saves us half the trouble ; and this probably gave rise to Plato's doctrine, that all learning is mere remembering.

As far as possible we ought to try and reduce all that we wish to incorporate in our memory to a perceptible image, either directly, or as an example, a mere simile, or an analogue, or indeed in any other way ; because intuitive perceptions take a far firmer hold than any abstract thoughts, let alone mere words.   This is why we remember things we have ourselves experienced so much better than those of which we read.

CHAPTER VIII.

§ 46. *The Systematic Order.*

THE order of succession in which I have stated the various forms of the Principle of Sufficient Reason in this treatise, is not systematic; it has been chosen for the sake of greater clearness, in order first to present what is better known and least presupposes the rest. In this I have followed Aristotle's rule: καὶ μαθήσεως οὐκ ἀπὸ τοῦ πρώτου, καὶ τῆς τοῦ πράγματος ἀρχῆς ἐνίοτε ἀρκτέον, ἀλλ᾽ ὅθεν ῥᾷστ᾽ ἂν μάθοι (*et doctrina non a primo, ac rei principio aliquando inchoanda est, sed unde quis facilius discat*).[1] But the systematic order in which the different classes of reasons ought to follow one another is the following. First of all should come The Principle of Sufficient Reason of Being; and in this again first its application to Time, as being the simple schema containing only what is essential in all the other forms of the Principle of Sufficient Reason, nay, as being the prototype of all finitude. The Reason of Being in Space having next been stated, the Law of Causality would then follow; after which would come the Law of Motives, and last of all the Principle of Sufficient Reason of Knowing; for the other classes of reasons refer to imme-

---

[1] Aristot. "Metaph." iv. 1. "Sometimes too, learning must start, not from what is really first and with the actual beginning of the thing concerned, but from where it is easiest to learn." [Tr.'s add.

diate representations, whereas this last class refers to representations derived from other representations.

The truth expressed above, that Time is the simple scheme which merely contains the essential part of all the forms of the Principle of Sufficient Reason, explains the absolutely perfect clearness and precision of Arithmetic, a point in which no other science can compete with it. For all sciences, being throughout combinations of reasons and consequences, are based upon the Principle of Sufficient Reason. Now, the series of numbers is the simple and only series of reasons and consequences of Being in Time ; on account of this perfect simplicity—nothing being omitted, no indefinite relations left—this series leaves nothing to be desired as regards accuracy, apodeictic certainty and clearness. All the other sciences yield precedence in this respect to Arithmetic; even Geometry : because so many relations arise out of the three dimensions of Space, that a comprehensive synopsis of them becomes too difficult, not only for pure, but even for empirical intuition; complicated geometrical problems are therefore only solved by calculation ; that is, Geometry is quick to resolve itself into Arithmetic. It is not necessary to point out the existence of sundry elements of obscurity in the other sciences.

§ 47. *Relation in Time between Reason and Consequence.*

According to the laws of causality and of motivation, a reason must precede its consequence in Time. That this is absolutely essential, I have shown in my chief work, to which I here refer my readers [1] in order to avoid repeating myself. Therefore, if we only bear in mind that it is not one thing which is the cause of another thing, but one state which is the cause of another state, we shall not

[1] See " Die Welt a. W. u. V.," vol. ii. ch. iv. p. 41, 42 of the 2nd edition, and p. 44 of the 3rd.

allow ourselves to be misled by examples like that given
by Kant,[1] that the stove, which is the cause of the
warmth of the room, is simultaneous with its effect. The
state of the stove: that is, its being warmer than its sur-
rounding medium, must precede the communication of its
surplus caloric to that medium ; now, as each layer of air
on becoming warm makes way for a cooler layer rushing
in, the first state, the cause, and consequently also the
second, the effect, are renewed until at last the temperature
of stove and room become equalized. Here therefore we
have no permanent cause (the stove) and permanent effect
(the warmth of the room) as simultaneous things, but a
chain of changes; that is, a constant renewing of two states,
one of which is the effect of the other. From this example,
however, it is obvious that even Kant's conception of
Causality was far from clear.

On the other hand, the Principle of Sufficient Reason of
Knowing conveys with it no relation in Time, but merely
a relation for our Reason : here therefore, *before* and *after*
have no meaning.

In the Principle of Sufficient Reason of Being, so far
as it is valid in Geometry, there is likewise no relation in
Time, but only a relation in Space, of which we might say
that all things were co-existent, if here the words coexistence and succession had any meaning. In Arithmetic,
on the contrary, the Reason of Being is nothing else but
precisely the relation of Time itself.

§ 48. *Reciprocity of Reasons.*

Hypothetical judgments may be founded upon the
Principle of Sufficient Reason in each of its significations, as

[1] Kant, "Krit. d. r. Vern.," 1st edition, p. 202 ; 5th edition, p. 248
(English translation by M. Müller, p. 177.)

indeed every hypothetical judgment is ultimately based
upon that principle, and here the laws of hypothetical
conclusions always hold good: that is to say, it is right
to infer the existence of the consequence from the existence
of the reason, and the non-existence of the reason from
the non-existence of the consequence; but it is wrong to
infer the non-existence of the consequence from the non-
existence of the reason, and the existence of the reason
from the existence of the consequence. Now it is singular
that in Geometry we are nevertheless nearly always able
to infer the existence of the reason from the existence
of the consequence, and the non-existence of the consequence from the non-existence of the reason. This proceeds, as I have shown in § 37, from the fact that, as each
line determines the position of the rest, it is quite indifferent which we begin at: that is, which we consider as the
reason, and which as the consequence. We may easily
convince ourselves of this by going through the whole of
the geometrical theorems. It is only where we have to do
not only with figures, *i.e.*, with the positions of lines, but
with planes independently of figures, that we find it in
most cases impossible to infer the existence of the reason
from the existence of the consequence, or, in other words,
to convert the propositions by making the condition the
conditioned. The following theorem gives an instance of
this: Triangles whose lengths and bases are equal, include
equal areas. This cannot be converted as follows: Triangles
whose areas are equal, have likewise equal bases and
lengths; for the lengths may stand in inverse proportion
to the bases.

In § 20 it has already been shown, that the law of
causality does not admit of reciprocity, since the effect
never can be the cause of its cause; therefore the conception of reciprocity is, in its right sense, inadmissible.
Reciprocity, according to the Principle of Sufficient Reason

of knowing, would only be possible between equivalent conceptions, since the spheres of these alone cover each other mutually. Apart from these, it only gives rise to a vicious circle.

§ 49. *Necessity.*

The Principle of Sufficient Reason in all its forms is the sole principle and the sole support of all necessity. For *necessity* has no other true and distinct meaning than that of the infallibility of the consequence when the reason is posited. Accordingly every necessity is *conditioned :* absolute, *i.e.*, unconditioned, necessity therefore is a *contradicto in adjecto.* For *to be necessary* can never mean anything but to result from a given reason. By defining it as "what cannot not be," on the other hand, we give a mere verbal definition, and screen ourselves behind an extremely abstract conception to avoid giving a definition of the thing. But it is not difficult to drive us from this refuge by inquiring how the non-existence of anything can be possible or even conceivable, since all existence is only given empirically. It then comes out, that it is only possible so far as some *reason* or other is posited or present, from which it follows. To be necessary and to follow from a given reason, are thus convertible conceptions, and may always, as such, be substituted one for the other. The conception of an "ABSOLUTELY *necessary Being* " which finds so much favour with pseudo-philosophers, contains therefore a contradiction : it annuls by the predicate "*absolute* " (*i.e.*, "unconditioned by anything else ") the only determination which makes the "*necessary* " conceivable. Here again we have an instance of the *improper use of abstract conceptions* to play off a metaphysical artifice such as those I have already pointed out in the conceptions "*immaterial substance,*" "*cause in general,*" "*absolute reason,*"

&c. &c.[1] I can never insist too much upon all abstract
conceptions being checked by *perception*.

There exists accordingly a *fourfold* necessity, in conformity with the *four* forms of the Principle of Sufficient
Reason :—

1°. *Logical necessity*, according to the principle of sufficient
reason of knowing, in virtue of which, when once we have
admitted the premisses, we must absolutely admit the
conclusion.

2°. *Physical necessity*, according to the law of causality,
in virtue of which, as soon as the cause presents itself, the
effect must infallibly follow.

3°. *Mathematical necessity*, according to the principle of
sufficient reason of being, in virtue of which, every relation
which is stated in a true geometrical theorem, is as that
theorem affirms it to be, and every correct calculation
remains irrefutable.

4°. *Moral necessity*, in virtue of which, every human
being, every animal even, is *compelled*, as soon as a motive
presents itself, to do that which alone is in accordance
with the inborn and immutable character of the individual.
This action now follows its cause therefore as infallibly as
every other effect, though it is less easy here to predict
what that effect will be than in other cases, because of the
difficulty we have in fathoming and completely knowing
the individual empirical character and its allotted sphere
of knowledge, which is indeed a very different thing from
ascertaining the chemical properties of a neutral salt and
predicting its reaction. I must repeat this again and
again on account of the dunces and blockheads who, in
defiance of the unanimous authority of so many great

---

[1] Compare " Die Welt a. W. u. V.," vol. i. p. 551 *et seq.* of the 2nd
edition (i. p. 582 *et seq.* of 3rd edition) as to " immaterial substance,"
and § 52 of the present work as to " reason in general." (Editor's
note.)

thinkers, still persist in audaciously maintaining the contrary, for the benefit of their old woman's philosophy. I am not a professor of philosophy, forsooth, that I need bow to the folly of others.

§ 50. *Series of Reasons and Consequences.*

According to the law of causality, the condition is itself always conditioned, and, moreover, conditioned in the same way; therefore, there arises a series *in infinitum a parte ante.* It is just the same with the Reason of Being in Space : each relative space is a figure ; it has its limits, by which it is connected with another relative space, and which themselves condition the figure of this other, and so on throughout all dimensions *in infinitum.* But when we examine a single figure in itself, the series of reasons of being has an end, because we start from a given relation, just as the series of causes comes to an end if we stop at pleasure at any particular cause. In Time, the series of reasons of being has infinite extension both *a parte ante,* and *a parte post,* since each moment is conditioned by a preceding one, and necessarily gives rise to the following. Time has therefore neither beginning nor end. On the other hand, the series of reasons of knowledge—that is, a series of judgments, each of which gives logical truth to the other—always ends somewhere, *i.e.,* either in an empirical, a transcendental, or a metalogical truth. If the reason of the major to which we have been led is an empirical truth, and we still continue asking *why,* it is no longer a reason of knowledge that is asked for, but a cause—in other words, the series of reasons of knowing passes over into the series of reasons of becoming. But if we do the contrary, that is, if we allow the series of reasons of becoming to pass over into the series of reasons of knowing, in order to bring it to an end, this is never brought about by the nature of the thing, but always by a special purpose: it is therefore a trick, and this is the sophism known by the name of the Ontological Proof. For when a cause, at which it seems desirable to stop short in order to make it the *first* cause, has been reached by means of the Cosmological Proof, we find out that the law of causality is not so easily brought to a standstill, and still persists in asking *why*: so it is simply set aside and the principle of sufficient reason of knowing, which from a distance resembles it, is substituted in its stead; and thus a reason of knowledge is given in the place of the cause which had been asked for—a reason of knowledge derived from the conception itself which has to be demonstrated, the reality of which is therefore still problematical: and this reason, as after all it is one, now has to figure as a cause. Of course the conception itself has been previously arranged for this purpose, and reality slightly covered with a few husks just for decency's sake has been placed within it, so as to give the delightful surprise of finding it there—as has been shown in Section 7. On the other hand, if a chain of judgments ultimately rests upon a principle of transcendental or of metalogical truth, and we still continue to ask *why*, we receive no answer at all, because the question has no meaning, *i.e.*, it does not know what kind of reason it is asking for.

For the Principle of Sufficient Reason is the *principle of all explanation: to explain a thing* means, to reduce its given existence or connection to some form or other of the Principle of Sufficient Reason, in accordance with which form that existence or connection necessarily is that which it is. The Principle of Sufficient Reason itself, *i.e.*, the connection expressed by it in any of its forms, cannot therefore be further explained; because there exists no principle by which to explain the source of all explanation: just as the eye is unable to see itself, though it sees everything else. There are of course series of motives, since the resolve to attain an end becomes the motive for the resolve to use a whole series of means; still this series invariably ends *à parte priori* in a representation belonging to one of our two first classes, in which lies the motive which originally had the power to set this individual will in motion. The fact that it was able to do this, is a datum for knowing the empirical character here given, but it is impossible to answer the question why that particular motive acts upon that particular character; because the intelligible character lies outside Time and never becomes an Object. Therefore the series of motives, as such, finds its termination in some such final motive and, according to the nature of its last link, passes into the series of causes, or that of reasons of knowledge: that is to say, into the former, when that last link is a real object; into the latter, when it is a mere conception.

§ 51. *Each Science has for its Guiding Thread one of the Forms of the Principle of Sufficient Reason in preference to the others.*

As the question *why* always demands a sufficient reason, and as it is the connection of its notions according to the principle of sufficient reason which distinguishes science from a mere aggregate of notions, we have called that *why* the parent of all science (§ 4). In each science, moreover, we find one of the forms of that principle predominating over the others as its guiding-thread. Thus in pure Mathematics the reason of being is the chief guiding-thread (although the exposition of the proofs proceeds according to the reason of knowing only); in applied Mathematics the law of causality appears together with it, but in Physics, Chemistry, Geology, &c., that law entirely predominates. The principle of sufficient reason in knowing finds vigorous application throughout all the sciences, for in all of them the particular is known through the general; but in Botany, Zoology, Mineralogy, and other classifying sciences, it is the chief guide and predominates absolutely. The law of motives (*motivation*) is the chief guide in History, Politics, Pragmatic Psychology, &c. &c., when we consider all motives and maxims, whatever they may be, as data for explaining actions—but when we make those motives and maxims the object-matter of investigation from the point of view of their value and origin, the law of motives becomes the guide to Ethics. In my chief work will be found the highest classification of the sciences according to this principle.[1]

§ 52. *Two principal Results.*

I have endeavoured in this treatise to show that the Principle of Sufficient Reason is a common expression for four completely different relations, each of which is founded upon a particular law given *à priori* (the principle of sufficient reason being a synthetical *à priori* principle). Now, according to the principle of *homogeneity*, we are compelled to assume that these four laws, discovered according to the principle of specification, as they agree in being expressed by one and the same term, must necessarily spring from one and the same original quality of our whole cognitive faculty as their common root, which we should accordingly have to look upon as the innermost germ of all dependence, relativeness, instability and limitation of the objects of our consciousness—itself limited to Sensibility, Understanding, Reason, Subject and Object—or of that world, which the divine Plato repeatedly degrades to the ἀεὶ γιγνόμενον μὲν

---

[1] " Die Welt a. W. u. V.," vol. ii. ch. 12, p. 126 of the 2nd edition (p. 139 of the 3rd edition).

καὶ ἀπολλύμενον, ὄντως δὲ οὐδέποτε ὄν (ever arising and
perishing, but in fact never existing), the knowledge of
which is merely a δόξα μετ᾽ αἰσθήσεως ἀλόγου, and which
Christendom, with a correct instinct, calls *temporal*, after
that form of our principle (Time) which I have defined as
its simplest schema and the prototype of all limitation.
The general meaning of the Principle of Sufficient Reason
may, in the main, be brought back to this: that every
thing existing no matter when or where, exists *by reason of
something else.* Now, the Principle of Sufficient Reason is
nevertheless *à priori* in all its forms: that is, it has its root
in our intellect, therefore it must not be applied to the
totality of existent things, the Universe, including that intellect in which it presents itself. For a world like this,
which presents itself in virtue of *à priori* forms, is just on
that account mere phenomenon; consequently that which
holds good with reference to it as the result of these forms,
cannot be applied to the world itself, *i.e.* to the thing in
itself, representing itself in that world.   Therefore we cannot say, "the world and all things in it exist by reason of
something else;" and this proposition is precisely the Cosmological Proof.

If, by the present treatise, I have succeeded in deducing
the result just expressed, it seems to me that every speculative philosopher who founds a conclusion upon the Principle of Sufficient Reason or indeed talks of a reason at all,
is bound to specify which kind of reason he means.   One
might suppose that wherever there was any question of a
reason, this would be done as a matter of course, and that
all confusion would thus be impossible.   Only too often,
however, do we still find either the terms reason and cause
confounded in indiscriminate use; or do we hear basis and
what is based, condition and what is conditioned, *principia*
and *principiata* talked about in quite a *general* way without
any nearer determination, perhaps because there is a secret

consciousness that these conceptions are being used in an unauthorized way. Thus even Kant speaks of the thing in itself as the *reason*[1] of the phenomenon, and also of a *ground* of the *possibility* of all phenomena,[2] of an *intelligible cause* of phenomena, of an *unknown ground* of the possibility of the sensuous series in general, of a *transcendental object*[3] as the *ground* of all phenomena and of the *reason* why our sensibility should have this rather than all other supreme conditions, and so on in several places. Now all this does not seem to me to tally with those weighty, profound, nay immortal words of his,[4] "the contingency[5] of things is itself mere phenomenon, and can lead to no other than the empirical regressus which determines phenomena."

That since Kant the conceptions reason and consequence, *principium* and *principiatum*, &c. &c., have been and still are used in a yet more indefinite and even quite transcendent sense, everyone must know who is acquainted with the more recent works on philosophy.

The following is my objection against this promiscuous employment of the word *ground* (reason) and, with it, of the Principle of Sufficient Reason in general ; it is likewise the second result, intimately connected with the first, which the present treatise gives concerning its subject-matter proper. The four laws of our cognitive faculty, of which the Prin-

[1] Or *ground*.
[2] Kant, "Krit. d. r. Vern.," 1st edition, pp. 561, 562, 564; p. 590 of the 5th edition. (Pp. 483 to 486 of the English translation by M. Müller.)
[3] *Ibid.* p. 540 of 1st edition, and 641 of 5th edition. (P. 466 of English translation.)
[4] *Ibid.* p. 563 of the 1st and 591 of the 5th edition. (P. 485 of English translation.)
[5] Empirical contingency is meant, which, with Kant, signifies as much as dependence upon other things. As to this, I refer my readers to my censure in my "Critique of Kantian Philosophy," p. 524 of the 2nd, and p. 552 of the 3rd edition.

ciple of Sufficient Reason is the common expression, by their common character as well as by the fact that all Objects for the Subject are divided amongst them, proclaim themselves to be posited by one and the same primary quality and inner peculiarity of our knowing faculty, which faculty manifests itself as Sensibility, Understanding, and Reason. Therefore, even if we imagined it to be possible for a new Fifth Class of Objects to come about, we should in that case likewise have to assume that the Principle of Sufficient Reason would appear in this class also under a different form. Notwithstanding all this, we still have no right to talk of an *absolute reason* (ground), nor does a *reason in general*, any more than a *triangle in general*, exist otherwise than as a conception derived by means of discursive reflection, nor is this conception, as a representation drawn from other representations, anything more than a means of thinking several things in one. Now, just as every triangle must be either acute-angled, right-angled, or obtuse-angled, and either equilateral, isosceles or scalene, so also must every reason belong to one or other of the four possible kinds of reasons I have pointed out. Moreover, since we have only four well-distinguished Classes of Objects, every reason must also belong to one or other of these four, and no further Class being possible, Reason itself is forced to rank it within them; for as soon as we employ a reason, we presuppose the Four Classes as well as the faculty of representing (*i.e.* the whole world), and must hold ourselves within these bounds, never transcending them. Should others, however, see this in a different light and opine that a *reason in general* is anything but a conception, derived from the four kinds of reasons, which expresses what they all have in common, we might revive the controversy of the Realists and Nominalists, and then I should side with the latter.

GREAT MINDS PAPERBACK SERIES

ART

❏ Leonardo da Vinci—*A Treatise on Painting*

ECONOMICS

❏ Charlotte Perkins Gilman—*Women and Economics: A Study of the Economic Relation between Women and Men*
❏ John Maynard Keynes—*The End of Laissez-Faire* and *The Economic Consequences of the Peace*
❏ John Maynard Keynes—*The General Theory of Employment, Interest, and Money*
❏ John Maynard Keynes—*A Tract on Monetary Reform*
❏ Thomas R. Malthus—*An Essay on the Principle of Population*
❏ Alfred Marshall—*Money, Credit, and Commerce*
❏ Alfred Marshall—*Principles of Economics*
❏ Karl Marx—*Theories of Surplus Value*
❏ John Stuart Mill—*Principles of Political Economy*
❏ David Ricardo—*Principles of Political Economy and Taxation*
❏ Adam Smith—*Wealth of Nations*
❏ Thorstein Veblen—*The Theory of the Leisure Class*

HISTORY

❏ Edward Gibbon—*On Christianity*
❏ Alexander Hamilton, John Jay, and James Madison—*The Federalist*
❏ Herodotus—*The History*
❏ Charles Mackay—*Extraordinary Popular Delusions and the Madness of Crowds*
❏ Thucydides—*History of the Peloponnesian War*

LAW

❏ John Austin—*The Province of Jurisprudence Determined*

LITERATURE

❏ Jonathan Swift—*A Modest Proposal and Other Satires*
❏ H. G. Wells—*The Conquest of Time*

POLITICS

❏ Walter Lippmann—*A Preface to Politics*

PSYCHOLOGY

❏ Sigmund Freud—*Totem and Taboo*

RELIGION/FREETHOUGHT

❏ Desiderius Erasmus—*The Praise of Folly*
❏ Thomas Henry Huxley—*Agnosticism and Christianity and Other Essays*
❏ Ernest Renan—*The Life of Jesus*
❏ Upton Sinclair—*The Profits of Religion*
❏ Elizabeth Cady Stanton—*The Woman's Bible*

❑ Voltaire—*A Treatise on Toleration and Other Essays*
❑ Andrew D. White—*A History of the Warfare of Science
with Theology in Christendom*

SCIENCE

❑ Jacob Bronowski—*The Identity of Man*
❑ Nicolaus Copernicus—*On the Revolutions of Heavenly Spheres*
❑ Francis Crick—*Of Molecules and Men*
❑ Marie Curie—*Radioactive Substances*
❑ Charles Darwin—*The Autobiography of Charles Darwin*
❑ Charles Darwin—*The Descent of Man*
❑ Charles Darwin—*The Origin of Species*
❑ Charles Darwin—*The Voyage of the* Beagle
❑ René Descartes—*Treatise of Man*
❑ Albert Einstein—*Relativity*
❑ Michael Faraday—*The Forces of Matter*
❑ Galileo Galilei—*Dialogues Concerning Two New Sciences*
❑ Francis Galton—*Hereditary Genius*
❑ Ernst Haeckel—*The Riddle of the Universe*
❑ William Harvey—*On the Motion of the Heart and Blood in Animals*
❑ Werner Heisenberg—*Physics and Philosophy:
The Revolution in Modern Science*
❑ Fred Hoyle—*Of Men and Galaxies*
❑ Julian Huxley—*Evolutionary Humanism*
❑ Thomas H. Huxley—*Evolution and Ethics* and *Science and Morals*
❑ Edward Jenner—*Vaccination against Smallpox*
❑ Johannes Kepler—*Epitome of Copernican Astronomy
and Harmonies of the World*
❑ James Clerk Maxwell—*Matter and Motion*
❑ Isaac Newton—*Opticks, Or Treatise of the Reflections,
Inflections, and Colours of Light*
❑ Isaac Newton—*The Principia*
❑ Louis Pasteur and Joseph Lister—*Germ Theory and Its Applications
to Medicine* and *On the Antiseptic Principle of the Practice of Surgery*
❑ William Thomson (Lord Kelvin) and Peter Guthrie Tait—
The Elements of Natural Philosophy
❑ Alfred Russel Wallace—*Island Life*

SOCIOLOGY

❑ Emile Durkheim—*Ethics and the Sociology of Morals*

GREAT BOOKS IN PHILOSOPHY PAPERBACK SERIES

ESTHETICS

❑ Aristotle—*The Poetics*
❑ Aristotle—*Treatise on Rhetoric*

ETHICS

❑ Aristotle—*The Nicomachean Ethics*
❑ Marcus Aurelius—*Meditations*
❑ Jeremy Bentham—*The Principles of Morals and Legislation*

❏ John Dewey—*Human Nature and Conduct*
❏ John Dewey—*The Moral Writings of John Dewey, Revised Edition*
❏ Epictetus—*Enchiridion*
❏ David Hume—*An Enquiry Concerning the Principles of Morals*
❏ Immanuel Kant—*Fundamental Principles of the Metaphysic of Morals*
❏ John Stuart Mill—*Utilitarianism*
❏ George Edward Moore—*Principia Ethica*
❏ Friedrich Nietzsche—*Beyond Good and Evil*
❏ Plato—*Protagoras, Philebus,* and *Gorgias*
❏ Bertrand Russell—*Bertrand Russell On Ethics, Sex, and Marriage*
❏ Arthur Schopenhauer—*The Wisdom of Life* and *Counsels and Maxims*
❏ Adam Smith—*The Theory of Moral Sentiments*
❏ Benedict de Spinoza—*Ethics* including
   The Improvement of the Understanding

LOGIC

❏ George Boole—*The Laws of Thought*

METAPHYSICS/EPISTEMOLOGY

❏ Aristotle—*De Anima*
❏ Aristotle—*The Metaphysics*
❏ Francis Bacon—*Essays*
❏ George Berkeley—*Three Dialogues Between Hylas and Philonous*
❏ W. K. Clifford—*The Ethics of Belief and Other Essays*
❏ René Descartes—*Discourse on Method* and *The Meditations*
❏ John Dewey—*How We Think*
❏ John Dewey—*The Influence of Darwin on Philosophy and Other Essays*
❏ Epicurus—*The Essential Epicurus: Letters, Principal Doctrines,
   Vatican Sayings, and Fragments*
❏ Sidney Hook—*The Quest for Being*
❏ David Hume—*An Enquiry Concerning Human Understanding*
❏ David Hume—*A Treatise on Human Nature*
❏ William James—*The Meaning of Truth*
❏ William James—*Pragmatism*
❏ Immanuel Kant—*The Critique of Judgment*
❏ Immanuel Kant—*Critique of Practical Reason*
❏ Immanuel Kant—*Critique of Pure Reason*
❏ Gottfried Wilhelm Leibniz—*Discourse on Metaphysics* and the *Monadology*
❏ John Locke—*An Essay Concerning Human Understanding*
❏ George Herbert Mead—*The Philosophy of the Present*
❏ Michel de Montaigne—*Essays*
❏ Charles S. Peirce—*The Essential Writings*
❏ Plato—*The Euthyphro, Apology, Crito,* and *Phaedo*
❏ Plato—*Lysis, Phaedrus,* and *Symposium*
❏ Bertrand Russell—*The Problems of Philosophy*
❏ George Santayana—*The Life of Reason*
❏ Arthur Schopenhauer—*On the Principle of Sufficient Reason*
❏ Sextus Empiricus—*Outlines of Pyrrhonism*
❏ Alfred North Whitehead—*The Concept of Nature*
❏ Ludwig Wittgenstein—*Wittgenstein's Lectures: Cambridge, 1932–1935*

PHILOSOPHY OF RELIGION

- ❏ Jeremy Bentham—*The Influence of Natural Religion on the Temporal Happiness of Mankind*
- ❏ Marcus Tullius Cicero—*The Nature of the Gods* and *On Divination*
- ❏ Ludwig Feuerbach—*The Essence of Christianity*
- ❏ Ludwig Feuerbach—*The Essence of Religion*
- ❏ Paul Henri Thiry, Baron d'Holbach—*Good Sense*
- ❏ David Hume—*Dialogues Concerning Natural Religion*
- ❏ William James—*The Varieties of Religious Experience*
- ❏ John Locke—*A Letter Concerning Toleration*
- ❏ Lucretius—*On the Nature of Things*
- ❏ John Stuart Mill—*Three Essays on Religion*
- ❏ Friedrich Nietzsche—*The Antichrist*
- ❏ Thomas Paine—*The Age of Reason*
- ❏ Bertrand Russell—*Bertrand Russell On God and Religion*

SOCIAL AND POLITICAL PHILOSOPHY

- ❏ Aristotle—*The Politics*
- ❏ Mikhail Bakunin—*The Basic Bakunin: Writings, 1869–1871*
- ❏ Edmund Burke—*Reflections on the Revolution in France*
- ❏ John Dewey—*Freedom and Culture*
- ❏ John Dewey—*Individualism Old and New*
- ❏ John Dewey—*Liberalism and Social Action*
- ❏ G. W. F. Hegel—*The Philosophy of History*
- ❏ G. W. F. Hegel—*Philosophy of Right*
- ❏ Thomas Hobbes—*The Leviathan*
- ❏ Sidney Hook—*Paradoxes of Freedom*
- ❏ Sidney Hook—*Reason, Social Myths, and Democracy*
- ❏ John Locke—*The Second Treatise on Civil Government*
- ❏ Niccolo Machiavelli—*The Prince*
- ❏ Karl Marx (with Friedrich Engels)—*The German Ideology*, including *Theses on Feuerbach* and *Introduction to the Critique of Political Economy*
- ❏ Karl Marx—*The Poverty of Philosophy*
- ❏ Karl Marx/Friedrich Engels—*The Economic and Philosophic Manuscripts of 1844* and *The Communist Manifesto*
- ❏ John Stuart Mill—*Considerations on Representative Government*
- ❏ John Stuart Mill—*On Liberty*
- ❏ John Stuart Mill—*On Socialism*
- ❏ John Stuart Mill—*The Subjection of Women*
- ❏ Montesquieu, Charles de Secondat—*The Spirit of Laws*
- ❏ Friedrich Nietzsche—*Thus Spake Zarathustra*
- ❏ Thomas Paine—*Common Sense*
- ❏ Thomas Paine—*Rights of Man*
- ❏ Plato—*Laws*
- ❏ Plato—*The Republic*
- ❏ Jean-Jacques Rousseau—*Émile*
- ❏ Jean-Jacques Rousseau—*The Social Contract*
- ❏ Bertrand Russell—*Political Ideals*
- ❏ Mary Wollstonecraft—*A Vindication of the Rights of Men*
- ❏ Mary Wollstonecraft—*A Vindication of the Rights of Women*